Why Does Patriarchy Persist?

Carol Gilligan
Naomi Snider

Why Does Patriarchy Persist?

Polity

The right of Carol Gilligan, Naomi Snider to be identified as Author of this Work has been asserted in accordance with the UK Copyright, Designs and Patents Act 1988.

First published in 2018 by Polity Press

Polity Press
65 Bridge Street
Cambridge CB2 1UR, UK

Polity Press
101 Station Landing
Suite 300
Medford, MA 02155, USA

ISBN-13: 978-1-5095-2912-4
ISBN-13: 978-1-5095-2913-1(pb)

A catalogue record for this book is available from the British Library.
Library of Congress Cataloging-in-Publication Data
Names: Gilligan, Carol, 1936- author. | Snider, Naomi, author.
Title: Why does patriarchy persist? / Carol Gilligan, Naomi Snider.
Description: Cambridge, UK ; Medford, MA, USA : Polity Press, [2018] | Includes bibliographical references and index.
Identifiers: LCCN 2018004124 (print) | LCCN 2018022965 (ebook) | ISBN 9781509529155 (Epub) | ISBN 9781509529124 | ISBN 9781509529131 (pbk.)
Subjects: LCSH: Patriarchy--Psychological aspects. | Social psychology.
Classification: LCC GN479.6 (ebook) | LCC GN479.6 .G56 2018 (print) | DDC 306--dc23
LC record available at https://lccn.loc.gov/2018004124

Typeset in 11 on 14 pt Sabon
by Fakenham Prepress Solution, Fakenham, Norfolk, NR21 8NN
Printed and bound in Great Britain by Clays Ltd, Popson Street, Bungay

For further information on Polity, visit our website: politybooks.com

Contents

Acknowledgments

This book had its inception in a seminar on resisting injustice, taught in the Fall of 2014 at the NYU School of Law. Its development was spurred by an invitation from the William Alanson White Institute to give a talk in their Fall colloquium series of 2016—a talk which as it turned out took place on the night following Trump's election. Reading the published version of our talk, John Thompson invited us to turn it into a book. We owe an immense debt of gratitude to David Richards who co-taught the seminar on resisting injustice, to Nancy Nereo who chaired the colloquium series at White, and to John Thompson of Polity Press. In crucial ways, they encouraged and supported our collaboration.

We are profoundly grateful as well to the students whose voices inform and illuminate our discoveries. Our thanks to Adam and Jackie especially, and also to Christine and Katie for their contributions to this book. Thanks also to the members of NYU's Radical Listening Project—Jacqueline Cruz, Jessica Eddy, Noor Jones-Bay, and Tonya Leslie for their careful reading of earlier drafts

Acknowledgments

of the manuscript. Their responses challenged us to think through more clearly many of the issues we raise. To Noor especially, our gratitude for her insights on the intersections of race and gender. To Ursula Diamond, Blythe Hawthorne-Loizeaux, and Dana Karin, our thanks for their responses to earlier phases of this work. Special thanks to Vice Provost Linda Mills. And to Beth Nash, special gratitude for her support of this project.

Our appreciation to Miri Abramis, Phillip Blumberg, Eugenio Duarte, Susan Fabrick, Sharon Kofman, Sue Kolod, Ruth Livingston, Gary Schlesinger, and Sarah Stemp of the White Institute for their contributions to this work. Our thanks to Tina Packer, Tova Hartman, Donna Kirshbaum, and Rachel Kadish, to Danielle Knafo, Beth Feldman, B. J. Cling, Judy Warren and Wendy Miller, and to Tracy Sidesinger, Tatyana Liskovich, and Schuyler Hunt—their responses to manuscript drafts were immensely helpful to us at various stages along the way. Special thanks to our readers for Polity Press for their wise suggestions.

Naomi wishes to thank Ruth Imber and James Phillips for listening, Elio Viglione for pushing her to places she had dared not go before, and Rachel Snider and Helen Snider for their constancy and love. She will always be grateful to her teachers—Carol and David Richards—for hearing and encouraging her protesting voice when it was just a whisper. Carol wishes to thank Dean Trevor Morrison for his support of this project in its early stages, and Peter Freedberger for his thoughtful assistance. She wants to thank John Thompson for his discerning eye and ongoing encouragement, and Jim Gilligan for being the ear she relies on.

Introduction

In the late fall of 2016, as Americans grappled with the election of Donald Trump as president, Adam, a third-year law student, turned inward. In his final paper for a seminar on resisting injustice, he puzzled over his betrayal of love. Ollie had been his best friend since they were six years old and played on the same soccer team. Adam recalls that over the years of their friendship they "became brothers," trusting each other with their most intimate secrets. He remembers being nine years old and confiding in Ollie his desire to audition for the solo in his school's fourth grade concert. This was the first time that Adam had revealed to anyone outside of his immediate family that he liked to sing. For him, a self-proclaimed "jock," the confession was a "pretty big deal. Rather than mock me, Ollie roped me into spending the whole day rehearsing the solo in front of him while we built a stage frame out of broken down cardboard boxes."

Yet starting in tenth grade, Adam writes, "I began to consciously distance myself from Ollie for the first time. Girls that I knew from his school had confirmed for me what I already suspected. Ollie was gay." In response, Adam began describing Ollie as "just a friend from soccer," as if the friendship had been "forced upon me by some great and unavoidable coincidence caused by sport and geographic location." Adam remembers telling his grandfather that he "used to have a best friend, but no longer did." By senior year of high school the two boys had "basically stopped communicating" and since then have "communicated exactly twice per year": sending a text on each other's birthday.

Looking back, Adam is struck that his decision to stop calling Ollie his best friend in tenth grade was more "prophetic than it was accurate at the time I said it. I had achieved exactly what I had set out to achieve. I had distanced myself from my best friend at a time when boys aren't supposed to have best friends anymore, and certainly not best friends who might be breaking the love laws." And yet, Adam felt an "overwhelming sense of sadness." It was not a bond Adam had wanted to break, and yet he had felt driven to do so:

> It was as if something was telling me that I needed to separate my mind and my emotions, but I wasn't aware of what exactly it was, and I wasn't going to rock the boat to find out what would happen if I didn't. In fact, I'm sure that I would have either rolled my eyes or laughed out loud if somebody had told me that the forces acting on me were forces pre-dating Aeschylus's 450 B.C.E. trilogy *The Oresteia*. In fact, I was being initiated into a framework of patriarchy and manhood without so much as a conscious thought about it. This is the problem with patriarchy. Its force, while massive,

is non-tangible, and its effects are both indirect and pervasive. Better said, the culprit is a ghost ...

Following the election of an unabashedly patriarchal man as president, what had been unconscious—done "without so much as a conscious thought"—became conscious. Adam was haunted by what he had done. The forces acting on him—an ancient framework of patriarchy and manhood—were intangible. Yet their effects were unmistakable. The love laws—Arundhati Roy's phrase for the laws that are a mainstay of patriarchy, the laws that "lay down who should be loved, and how. And how much"[1]—had led him to sacrifice his love for Ollie. "I loved and cared deeply for him. Ours was a brotherly love, familial rather than sexual, but it created a true bond that I did not want to break. And yet I acted in opposition to this impulse."

Jackie, a doctoral student in sociology, puzzled over her silence. As a senior at an elite college, she had been raped by one of her classmates, a man she had "known and lived with since freshman year." A man who up until this point she had considered a friend, but who had shown his "true colors" one night when he had forced himself on her despite her cries and repeated pleas for him to stop. The rape itself was not in question ("It was accepted that I was raped"). Yet as Jackie reflects in her final paper for the seminar on resisting injustice, she had felt pressured to "get 'over it,' to not make waves, to not ruin Tom's life." She went back to school and "kept my head down and my mouth shut. I didn't want to deal with it, I didn't want to be a rape victim, I didn't want to believe that someone I had known for over three years could be so careless." Jackie recognized that she "protected him at the expense of myself" by allowing him to continue living as if the rape had never happened. Why, she asks, had she heeded social mantras that would have her "not know what I knew"?

For Jackie too, the culprit was ghostlike: present yet non-corporeal, forceful yet intangible. The ghost was patriarchy. Its tell-tale marks were the codes of manhood and womanhood that had led Adam to break his bond with Ollie and Jackie to silence herself:

> My womanhood was both what allowed me to be objectified and raped, treated as male property, and also what was supposed to keep me silent: being a "good" girl and protecting men from their own "mistakes." When I reported my rape to the police, a year later, and the detective opened a drawer on other women who would never find justice, who were also told to be quiet, who the university made sure to silence (even after they reported!), I saw myself as part on a larger complex web of women. Despite racial or class differences, we were all victims to the notion that sexual violence was something that happened and that we would have to live with. I vowed in that detective's office to never be silent again.

Jackie had vowed no longer to comply with the forces that justify men's violence and women's silence, and yet she continued to puzzle over why she had complied with them in the first place.

An obvious answer is that there are consequences to not complying. Patriarchal codes of masculine honor and feminine goodness have been culturally sanctioned and socially enforced. They also have been taken as natural, so that breaking these codes appears unnatural, or at least not what a real man or a good woman would do. Yet Adam and Jackie prompt us to ask: is there also a psychology at work here, driving Adam to separate his mind from his emotions and thus not to think about what he is feeling and Jackie to not know what she knew? In essence, we are asking: does patriarchy also have a psychological function, protecting us from emotions and knowledge that have come to feel dangerous or unbearable, and is this in part why we continue to embrace it?

With the election of Donald Trump, the persistence of patriarchy has once again come to the fore as a question that calls for explanation. Why does patriarchy persist?

But first, what is patriarchy? Tolstoy describes a force that is crude, powerful and mysterious in its ability to turn what seems natural and good (love and feelings of tender compassion) into something that in the eyes of the world appears shameful and improper. In an often overlooked passage in *Anna Karenina*, Karenin, Anna's husband, an officious bureaucrat who is seemingly incapable of human feelings, "had given himself for the first time in his life to that feeling of tender compassion which other people's suffering evoked in him and which he had previously been ashamed of as a bad weakness."[2] Yet beside this "good spiritual force that had guided his soul, there was another force, crude and equally powerful, if not more so, that guided his life."[3] He knew beforehand that "everything was against him and that he would not be allowed to do what now seemed to him so natural and good but would be forced to do what was bad but seemed to them the proper thing."[4]

This depiction strikes us as apt. We define patriarchy as a culture based on a gender binary and hierarchy, a framework or lens that:

1. Leads us to see human capacities as either "masculine" or "feminine" and to privilege the masculine.
2. Elevates some men over other men and all men over women.
3. Forces a split between the self and relationships so that in effect men have selves, whereas women ideally are selfless, and women have relationships, which surreptitiously serve men's needs.

Patriarchy is an age-old structure that has been near universal, and yet there is an incoherence at its center because in reality men can't have selves without relationships and women can't have relationships without a self. Thus, in essence, patriarchy harms both men and women by forcing men to act as if they don't have or need relationships and women to act as if they don't have or need a self. But you're not supposed to see or to say this.

As a culture then, patriarchy exists as a set of rules and values, codes and scripts that specify how men and women should act and be in the world. Breaking these rules can have real consequences. More insidiously, patriarchy also exists internally, shaping how we think and feel, how we perceive and judge ourselves, our desires, our relationships and the world we live in. Moreover, these two aspects, the cultural and the psychological, often exist in a state of tension: we can unconsciously absorb and reify a framework that we consciously and actively oppose. In a paper entitled "The Nasty Woman: Destruction and the Path to Mutual Recognition," written shortly after Trump's election, the psychologist Tracy Sidesinger observes the ghost-like presence of patriarchal norms and values: "Even as we have developed conscious attitudes of equality, there is a much larger context of unconscious ideas of what women should be that hovers like a ghost, making the transformation to mutuality between masculine and feminine subjectivities much harder than we think it should be."[5] We can believe in a woman's equality and yet, as women, feel guilt when we put our own needs forward or uncomfortable when other women do the same, just as men, including feminist men, can feel anger and shame when their sense of autonomy or their status and power are threatened and their vulnerability exposed.

Thus Adam in fact—a phrase he repeats as if to underscore that it was in fact a fact—did not act on his impulse to maintain his true bond with Ollie, and Jackie, at least for a time, acceded to the pressures on her not to make waves or ruin Tom's life by saying what by his own admission was true: he had, in fact, raped her. The forces acting on them—both external and internal—had led them to sacrifice relationship, whether by betraying love or silencing themselves, and to maintain the hierarchy that elevates masculine over feminine, straight over gay, man over woman.

For Adam and Jackie the benefits of compliance were clear, but so too were the costs. To have stayed in close relationship with Ollie, Adam would have risked being labelled "gay" or seen as not a "real" man, yet by foregoing that connection in the name of manhood, Adam had sacrificed what he loved, something of infinite value. If Jackie had stayed with herself and spoken out about her rapist, she would have risked being called uncaring or seen as selfish in her willingness to "ruin his life," yet for Jackie her silence felt like "drowning" and a "betrayal of everything I had ever believed in." In asking why patriarchy persists, we are asking why a set of cultural rules and assumptions that are psychologically incoherent and harmful has such a powerful grip on the psyche? In essence, we are asking where is the resistance?

To put it more starkly, the willingness to override not only the voice of desire but also the voice of experience adds a psychological dimension to what has been the more common, political understanding as to why patriarchy is still a force we contend with. In addition to the realities of privilege and power, we are also dealing here with ghost-like forces that operate outside our awareness—with an initiation that bypasses conscious thought. Or, as Tolstoy dramatizes it in his novel, we are contending with a shift in the framework that makes what is bad seem good and what is natural and good feel shameful.

We recognize that there are complex social and political forces which can account for the persistence of patriarchy. Some people benefit from its institutional and economic arrangements and have a collective interest in maintaining them. Yet any political or social theory rests on a psychology: a set of assumptions about what people want and what drives them.

Introduction

Our work began with a question: does patriarchy persist not only because those in positions of power are loath to give up their privilege but also because it has a psychological function? By requiring a sacrifice of love for the sake of hierarchy (think of Abraham commanded by God to sacrifice his son Isaac), patriarchy steels us against the vulnerability of loving and by doing so, becomes a defense against loss. In this light, we suggest that forces outside our awareness may be driving a politics that otherwise appear inexplicable to many people.

This understanding then implies that psychological dynamics also may drive the backlash against any progress toward equality. Any dismantling of patriarchy poses a threat not simply to status and power, but to psychological defenses that protect us from what have become some of our deepest fears and most shameful desires. From this perspective we can begin, perhaps, to understand the rage and violence that so often follow when the mask of masculine invulnerability and autonomy slips and a man's desire for love or his need for care is exposed, and also why it is that some women shun women who speak from a place of their own desire and agency.

To lay the groundwork for what follows, we start with the evidence that, despite claims to the contrary, patriarchy is in fact not natural to us as humans. By nature, we are relational beings, born with a voice—the ability to communicate our experience—and with the desire to engage responsively with others. There is a growing consensus among those who study evolutionary history that our capacity for mutual understanding— for empathy, mind-reading, and cooperation—was key to our evolutionary success and responsible for our survival as a species.[6] From an evolutionary standpoint, patriarchy posed a threat. To put it starkly, in the words of the evolutionary anthropologist Sarah Blaffer Hrdy, "patriarchal ideologies that focused on both the chastity of women and the perpetuation and augmentation of male lineages undercut the long-standing priority of putting children's well-being first."[7]

With this observation, traditional explanations as to why patriarchy persists, which focus solely on the advantages of status, wealth, and power, become suspect. If the desire for domination is not in fact natural, or at the very least conflicts with our natural relationality, why do we sacrifice the pleasures and benefits of human connection for the material advantages and the sense of superiority that come with social status and power? The question becomes even more complex once we recognize that a system of domination doesn't necessarily nullify or override what are basic human capacities. In fact our relational abilities (empathy, mind-reading, and cooperation) carry with them the power to override hierarchy. History is replete with examples of people who, even in the face of real terror, act out of love and in recognition of a common humanity. Risking their own lives and the safety of their family, Antonina Zabinska, the zookeeper's wife in occupied Warsaw, hid over 300 Jews in the zoo in the center of the city while Jan Zabinski, the zookeeper, devised a ruse that enabled him to lead Jews out of the ghetto under the eyes of the Nazis. When Jan was asked how they came to do what they did, he explained, "It was not an act of heroism, just a simple human obligation."[8]

Introduction

The YouTube video of the psychologist Edward Tronick's two-minute "still-face experiment" offers a vivid and easily accessible demonstration of how tuned in we are as babies by showing how quickly an infant picks up and responds to changes in the relational weather.[9] At the opening of the film, we see a mother and her one-year-old baby engaged in responsive play, cooing and gesturing in an ongoing and pleasurable exchange. When following Tronick's instruction the mother becomes still-faced and stops responding to her baby, the baby instantly registers the loss of connection. She moves to re-engage her mother by repeating the sounds and gestures that had previously elicited her response. When the mother ignores her efforts and remains still-faced, we see pleasure drain from the baby's body and face. And then it becomes almost unbearable to watch as disorganization sets in and we hear a cadenced relational voice give way to a shrill, high-pitched screeching. Our relief is visceral when the two-minute still face interval ends and the mother responds to the baby's distress. Our breathing returns to its normal rhythm as we witness the mother repair the rupture in the relationship and see the baby reengage with her.

In this brief two-minute window, we can recognize how trust in relationships hinges on the discovery that ruptures can be repaired. As Tronick and his colleagues have shown, it is not the absence of ruptures or breaks in connection or the goodness of the mother per se that ensures the continuation of the relationship. Rather, it is the discovery on the part of mother and baby that they can find one another again after what, in the course of daily living, are the inevitable moments of losing touch.

11

The YouTube video of the still-face experiment is also instructive because in the baby's response to the rupture we see how a loss of pleasure and a change in voice signal the loss in connection. From this we learn that by paying attention to changes in posture and listening for shifts in voice, we can pick up and follow the moves in and out of relationship. When the baby's pleasure fades and her voice shifts we are witnessing the beginnings of her loss of hope that the rupture can be repaired and we see her move to disengage. Then we can see how, if the capacity to repair is itself under siege, if the move to repair ruptures in relationship is rendered futile or shamed, the loss of connection becomes seemingly irreparable.

Our ability to communicate our own feelings, and to pick up the feelings of others and thus to heal fractures in connection, threatens the structures of hierarchy. Feelings of empathy and tender compassion for another's suffering or humanity make it difficult to maintain or justify inequality. So long as those below are able to communicate their feelings and those on top are able to feel empathy we are inevitably pulled toward repairing the ruptures that all forms of hierarchy create. And so, our relational desires and capacities—our wish to connect with others and our ability to register their feelings and to communicate our own feelings and experience to them—have to be compromised or reined in, sacrificed or constrained to maintain an order of living contingent on dividing people into the superior and the inferior, the touchables and the untouchables, whether on the basis of race, gender, class, caste, religion, sexuality, you name it. To

Introduction

enforce the sacrifice of relationship necessary for establishing and maintaining hierarchies of power and status, it is necessary then to render protest ineffective and to subvert the capacity to repair.

Patriarchy persists in part because it does just this.

We were taken by surprise by three discoveries: first, that the codes and scripts of patriarchal manhood and womanhood—that is, the patriarchal construction of what it takes to be an honorable man or a good woman—correspond to what the psychologist John Bowlby identifies as pathological responses to loss; namely, emotional detachment and compulsive caregiving. Second, that the initiation into patriarchal manhood and womanhood subverts the ability to repair ruptures in relationship by enjoining a man to separate his mind from his emotions (and thus not to think about what he is feeling) and a woman to remain silent (and thus not to say what she knows). The script is all too familiar. Far more than an illustration of feminine and masculine styles of communication, it is a conversational template that exposes the rupture brought on by patriarchy:

She: I feel something is wrong; for this whole past week we've been out of touch with each other.

He: I don't know what you're talking about.

She: I feel we're just not seeing each other, not paying attention to what's going on between us.

He: You're always complaining about something.

She: No really, I'm trying to say...

He: Look. I'm doing what you asked me to do. I can't do everything.

Silence

He: Is there something you want?

She: Never mind.

Our third discovery came with the realization that resistance to internalizing the gender codes of patriarchy tracks the same trajectory as responses to loss: protest, and when protest proves ineffective, despair and then detachment. By subverting the capacity for repair, patriarchy impels us on the path to detachment—the defensive move out of relationships designed to protect us from a loss that has come to seem inevitable.

Thus we came to see how patriarchy persists in part by forcing a loss of relationship and then rendering the loss irreparable. Without the possibility for repair, love, a force of nature that has the power to uproot patriarchy, becomes sacrificed to protect us from the pain of loss. This sacrifice of love then serves the establishment of hierarchy and opens the way to its preservation.

Our thesis points to a paradox: we give up relationship in order to have "relationships," meaning a place within the patriarchal order. In this sense, with its gender codes and scripts dictating what a man or woman should do in order to be safe or protected (as Abraham is by God), patriarchy is at once a source of lost connection and a defense against further loss, a source of trauma and a defense against trauma. While this paradox may not make rational sense, it has a psychological logic. That is to say, psychological illnesses, by definition harmful, also can carry psychological advantages, termed by psychoanalysts "gains." This language helps us to see how patriarchy persists in part because it renders the loss of relationship irreparable, and as a consequence of this, the sacrifice of connection—otherwise a psychological harm—becomes a psychological "gain": we avoid the very thing we want—love—so as not to be vulnerable again to a loss that has come to feel inescapable and unbearable.

The language of gains also helps us to understand the relationship between the psychological drivers of patriarchy and the more obvious and commonly discussed external motivators—the social and financial benefits that patriarchy bestows on some people, who then don't want to give them up. Psychoanalysts distinguish between the external benefits of symptoms (e.g. the attention and care that those who are ill may receive), termed secondary gains, and the internal benefits, which drive the development of symptoms in the first place, termed primary gains, as for example the reduction in anxiety. Contrasting the two, Freud wrote:

> In civil life illness can be used as a screen to gloss over incompetence in one's profession or in competition with other people; while in the family it can serve as a means for sacrificing the other members and extorting proofs of their love or for imposing one's will upon them. All of this lies fairly near the surface; we sum it up in the term 'gain from illness' ... But there are other motives, that lie still deeper, for holding on to being ill, which are not so easily dealt with. But these cannot be understood without a fresh journey into psychological theory.[10]

Just as in the case of illness, there are lying near the surface clear reasons why patriarchy persists—the power and status accorded to those on top being the most obvious. Most theories of patriarchy have focused solely on these secondary (external) gains. However, just as Freud saw that there are deeper unconscious gains driving pathology, we have come to see that "there are other motives, that lie still deeper, for holding on" to patriarchy, motives that "cannot be understood without a fresh journey into psychological theory."

We recount the journey that led us to these insights as a dialogue because the interplay of our voices proved key to the discoveries we came to. Without Naomi's personal story of loss, we might never have connected the developmental research that Carol initiated with Bowlby's studies on loss and attachment. It was this connection that led us to the thesis that patriarchy persists in part because it forces a betrayal of love and then renders the loss irreparable. Without Carol's ear for different voices and her eye for resistance we might not have to come to see so precisely the mechanisms at work in perpetuating a patriarchal order and also the forces working against its continuation. It was the shock of the 2016 election that jolted us into writing this book in the hope that if we can understand the psychology driving patriarchy, including those forces that act on us without a conscious thought, we can avoid becoming like Oedipus and walking blindly into what otherwise may seem our fate.

PART ONE

The Puzzle

Carol: Our starting point was *The Birth of Pleasure*, the 2002 book in which I draw out the implications of a ten-year project on girls' development.[1] It was listening to girls narrate their experiences in coming of age that first led me to question whether separations that had been seen as desirable or natural, part of the normal course of development (the separation of the mind from the body, of thought from emotion, and of the self from relationships) are more accurately viewed as responses to an initiation. What cued me to see this as an initiation was the realization that girls were responding to a force that was coming from outside themselves. Hearing some girls name the crisis of connection they faced when they felt pressed to choose between having a voice or having relationships alerted me to the loss of relationship they were registering. What had seemed ordinary—having a voice and living in relationship—suddenly had become extraordinary. The resistance of some girls to making a choice that they recognized as a bad bargain as well as psychologically incoherent prompted me to ask: where is this choice coming from and who is it serving?

Iris, a high school senior, stated the quandary most succinctly: "If I were to say what I was feeling and thinking, no one would want to be with me, my voice would be too loud," adding by way of explanation, "But you have to have relationships." Something was forcing her to give up relationship—the experience of connecting with herself and with others—as the price for having "relationships"—set and scripted ways of relating that provide the semblance of connection but by requiring the disavowal of core aspects of herself block the possibility for actual connection. I asked what seemed the obvious question—"But if you are not saying what you are feeling and thinking, then where are *you* in these relationships?"—and, watching her face shadow, it became clear to me that she too saw the paradox.[2] Either way, she would lose relationship, either by saying what she was feeling and thinking and thus becoming someone no one would want to be with, or by not saying what she was feeling and thinking and thus becoming someone other than herself. The loss of connection was seemingly inescapable. Hence the crisis.

Iris was the valedictorian of her high school class; she had been admitted to the prestigious college that was her first choice. Celebrated by all, she lamented the bargain she had made. Yet in her eyes, this was the price one paid for having "relationships" and making one's way in the world.

Thus Iris forgoes relationship for "relationships." It is important to emphasize this distinction between relationship and "relationships," between the experience of connecting and the appearance of connection, and also to stress that this sacrifice of relationship is adaptive, culturally sanctioned and socially rewarded. Yet Iris registers the loss.

The research with girls prompted two questions: do boys experience a similar crisis of connection? And, does this crisis occur at an earlier point in their development? The latter question drew on over a century of research showing that adolescence for girls is marked by a sudden high incidence of signs of psychological distress whereas for boys a similarly heightened risk to their resiliency occurs in the transition from early to middle childhood, roughly between the ages of four and seven.[3] That these gender differences with respect to times of heightened threat to children's resiliency are still evident today can be taken as evidence for the persistence of patriarchy, which as an order of living predicated on a gender binary and hierarchy targets and affects boys and girls differently.

In a study remarkable for its precision of observation, Judy Chu documents the relational acuity of boys at age four and five.[4] Their emotional sensitivity and intelligence were manifest in their attentiveness, their articulateness, their authenticity and directness with one another and with her. Right from the outset, this relational astuteness was clear. On a day when Judy is sitting on the floor close to three boys who are playing quietly in the block corner, and says, in response to a teacher's question, that she is trying to learn about the boys, Jake—one of the three—asks her: "What *exactly* do you want to learn?" When Judy says she wants to learn what it's like to be a boy, Jake turns to consult Mike who says: "Do you think we should trust her?" Judy writes: "Jake glances in my direction, then turns to face Mike and, with a smile on his face, shakes his head slowly from side to side to indicate no." Why should they trust her? They barely know her. Another time when her presence catches the boys' attention—the first time she brings in a small, hand-held tape recorder—one of them asks her: "Why do you have that thing?" Judy explains and then records what follows: Picking up his friend's lingering discomfort, Dan moves to remedy the situation "by walking over to me, gently placing a white lace shawl (that he retrieved from the house area) over my head, and casually informing me, 'We're just going to pretend you're not here.'"[5]

Following this group of boys as they moved from pre-kindergarten through kindergarten and into first grade, Chu witnessed them becoming gradually more inattentive, more inarticulate, more inauthentic and indirect with one another and with her. They were becoming "boys" or how boys are often said to be. In *When Boys Become Boys*, her 2014 book, she chronicles an initiation whereby boys learn the codes of a masculinity contingent on the suppression of empathy and the hiding of vulnerability necessary for claiming superiority, and also for avoiding rejection. Without any formal instruction or ceremony, as if in response to a ghost-like presence, the boys in her study were enacting in their play the gender binaries and hierarchies of a patriarchal order, where masculinity is defined in opposition to and as the opposite of anything feminine, where being a boy means not being a girl or

20

like a girl, and where being a boy is linked with superiority, that is, with privilege and power.

Chu's study captures how, as the price of becoming one of the boys, some boys replace their relational presence (their attentiveness, authenticity, articulateness, and directness) with relational pretense and posturing. She notes that, paradoxically, by shielding their relational desires and sensitivities in their wish to become one of the boys, these boys are sacrificing relationship in order to have "relationships."[6] In effect, they are facing the same dilemma as Iris: if they were to say what they were feeling and thinking and thus to reveal their emotional sensitivity and their vulnerability, the others boys would not want to be with them because they would be perceived as not a real boy. Yet by concealing these aspects of themselves in order to be seen as one of the boys and not girly or gay, they render the closeness they are now seeking with other boys unattainable. Either way, the loss is inescapable. But Chu also highlights boys' resistance, showing how strategic four- and five-year-old boys can be in responding to the codes of masculinity and reminding us that in general boys "know more than they show."[7]

In *Deep Secrets: Boys' Friendships and the Crisis of Connection*, Niobe Way draws on her studies with adolescent boys to reveal the "hidden landscape of boys' friendships."[8] In doing so, she counters the myth that only girls desire and are capable of emotional intimacy. As her quotes from boys make abundantly clear, the relational desires and sensitivities observed by Chu in boys at four and five flower among boys at adolescence, joined now by a greater subjectivity and

21

capacity to reflect on what they are experiencing and what they are encountering. Across a wide diversity of cultures, boys in the early years of high school are exuberant in describing their best friendships with other boys, friends with whom they share deep secrets. As Justin, a fifteen year old in an urban public school, says: "[My best friend and I] love each other ... that's it ... you have this thing that is deep, so deep, it's within you ... sometimes two people can really, really understand each other and really have a trust, respect, and love for each other. It just happens, it's human nature."[9]

Boys' love for their best friends is experienced by them as natural and good. Yet by the end of high school, a majority of the boys in Way's studies no longer have a best friend. They speak about betrayal, of no longer trusting others with their secrets, and they dismiss the need for emotional intimacy. As Fernando explains, he is learning "how to be more of a man"[10] in a world where being a man means being self-reliant, emotionally stoic and independent.

In this way, through an initiation that begins with young boys around the time when they are entering school, that continues with girls as they reach adolescence and are becoming young women, and then replays among boys in adolescence when they are learning how to be a man, femininity comes to be associated with pseudo-relationships (and the silencing of self) and masculinity with pseudo-independence (and the shielding of relational desires and sensitivities)—two sides of the same coin in that both are moves of the self out of relationship designed paradoxically to facilitate having "relationships." This is what we mean by a loss of relationship: a loss of intimacy and connection, rather than a permanent physical separation per se. As with the baby in the YouTube video, the loss of relationship is signaled by a loss of pleasure and a change in voice. You can see it, you can feel it, you can hear it in observing children, in clinical settings, and in everyday life.

These are long-standing patterns: so old in fact that we have a myth—like the Oedipus myth, a story passed down through time and across cultures, but instead of showing the path leading to tragedy, it shows a way out of these patterns: a path of resistance. In place of the Oedipal triangle—father, mother, and son—we see a daughter, her lover, and his mother: Psyche, Eros, and Venus.[11] With this reconfiguration of the main actors in the drama, an alternative path opens, contingent initially on Psyche's protest against being treated as an object and hence her resistance to pseudo-relationships, and ultimately on Eros's protest against the loss of relationship and his resistance to pseudo-independence.

These ancient myths show that in fact we know both the way into patriarchy and also a way out. A part often left out or forgotten in retelling the Oedipus story, or placing it as the cornerstone of normal development as psychoanalysts have done, is that the Oedipus myth has its roots in trauma. Laius, the king, had sexually abused a boy. He was told by the oracle of Apollo that retribution would come in the next generation at the hands of his own son. The birth of Oedipus, Laius's son, then sets in motion a series of events that end in tragedy: a father willing to sacrifice his son in the interest of self-preservation, a mother complicit in

23

the act of wounding and abandoning her child. Then Oedipus walking blindly into his fate, killing his father, bedding and wedding his mother, a plague breaking out in the city, and Oedipus—after literally blinding himself—summoning his daughters to accompany him in his blindness. Jocasta, the Oedipal mother, maintains her silence to the end.[12] The chorus comments: "How could that queen whom Laius won ... Be silent when that act was done." When the truth of what had in fact been done to Oedipus starts to emerge, Jocasta pleads "For God's love, let us have no more questioning" and then she strangles herself.[13]

Oedipus is a story of trauma and loss, abuse and violence, blindness and silence. It is a mythic rendering of the tragedy that inheres in patriarchy. To take this myth as a template for the human condition, as Freud and others have done, to carry forward the name Oedipus while forgetting the origins of his story in trauma, holds the danger of regarding murder and incest as natural impulses rather than impulses that arise in the wake of abuse and abandonment. It holds the danger of mistaking the culture of men's violence and women's silence for nature.

Psyche, the adolescent girl, resists playing her part in this Oedipal drama. She resists becoming the "new Venus," a replica of Eros's idealized mother. She breaks Eros's prohibition on her seeing him or speaking about their love, the compact sealing their relationship, their intimacy and his vulnerability in blindness and silence. Because in broad daylight, in his public persona, Eros is Cupid, the naughty boy shooting his arrows, whereas in darkness, where Psyche knows him, he is responsive

24

to her and a tender lover. And when she defies his prohibition and decides to see for herself, when Psyche takes the lamp and discovers that despite what her sisters have told her she is not in fact living with a monster, she sees what she had known in darkness and in silence: Eros, her lover but also the one who had bound her to blindness and silence as the condition for his loving her, is a vulnerable young man.

You see the point. If a young woman resists the bans on her seeing and speaking about what she knows from experience about love, about herself, and about men, and if a young man, in the end, stops hiding his love—as Eros does in the course of the myth—then a story that was headed for tragedy turns into a journey of resistance and struggle that can end, as the myth of Psyche and Eros ends, with a marriage of equals and the birth of a daughter named Pleasure. That is, with the start of a new story.

Knowing that just as patriarchy is not natural it is also not inevitable or inescapable, only heightens the question: why does patriarchy persist? If love marks the path leading out of patriarchy, why do we turn away from love?

The First Clue: An Association to Loss

Naomi: In the fall of 2014, I came to New York University to do a Masters in Law. Enticed by the name, I enrolled in the seminar "Resisting Injustice," taught by Carol and Professor David Richards. In the week that we read *The Birth of Pleasure*, I was struck by the voices Carol recorded in that book: both the voices of adolescent girls—forced to choose between having voice or having relationships—and the voices of fathers—struggling to navigate what it means to be good dads to emotionally intelligent sons. Sons growing up in a society where, in the words of one father, "men are at risk if they look too vulnerable."[1] The standout voice for me was the one Carol has already mentioned: the voice of Iris, the high school senior who says: "If I were to say what I was feeling and thinking, no one would want to be with me, my voice would be too loud." It could have been taken from one of my therapy sessions.

I noticed in reading Carol's work my thoughts kept going back to my father, back to December 25, 1990, Christmas Day, five days before my fifth birthday, the day my father died. My first taste of loss, on this the day of gifts (a new doll's house and pink felt pajamas). It was a day I did not speak about for over twenty years, but if you listened carefully enough the loss could be heard in every false move, every burst of anger and self-doubt, and every act of self-denial, self-punishment, and self-hate in the years that followed. It was the shameful secret lurking within all my desperate attempts to hide and transform myself.

Death defies fairness and logic. It picks its victims at random with sometimes seemingly little regard for worth, wealth, age, sex, creed, or caste. Death defies our belief in our own ability to control love, life, and loss. At age five, I rejected this lesson in human fragility. There must be some reason my father is gone, it must have been someone's fault (mine?), and there must be some way to bring him back. I repressed my urge to talk about my father by holding on desperately to the belief that, as long as I remained silent, there remained a chance that he would come back. My voice carried with it the power to make my father's death real, my silence the power to undo it. In time, this childish fantasy faded and in its place emerged a realization that he was gone forever coupled with a determination to avoid further loss at any cost. My tools were: repression, control, compromise, constant monitoring of others and self-adjustment, committing to nothing and no one, always hiding and always pleasing. I partitioned parts of myself—my real thoughts, feelings, and desires— from my relationships, and by sacrificing connection, I avoided loss.

Once one parent has died the fear of losing another is all consuming and breathtakingly terrifying. I recall sleepless nights at friends' houses, kept awake by the fear that in my absence something terrible may have happened to my family. I remember supermarket trips morphing into living nightmares when, turning my back on my mother for just a moment, distracted perhaps by the shiny wrapper of a favorite treat, I would look back to find her suddenly gone, lost to the mammoth maze of the supermarket aisles. In those moments of frantic searching I would berate myself for taking my eye off the ball and allowing her to disappear. For I knew better. I knew that someone you love could be lost in the blink of an eye without so much as a goodbye. I knew that the back and forth of relationship, that experience of being in and out of touch, carried with it the possibility of losing touch forever. And knowing the dangers of letting go and looking away I knew that the only way to guarantee security was to sacrifice the freedom of intimacy. I knew that the only way never to lose something was to never have it.

This desperate desire to avoid loss at any cost lives on in the fear that grips me even now when a "dangerous" thought or feeling arises—a thought which could hurt another person's feelings, cause conflict, render me someone whom others don't want to be with. The panic of loss arises and forces the thought to flutter away, to be replaced in my mouth—like a ventriloquist's dummy—with not my own words but the words I think that the other person wants to hear. The sadness that accompanies this compromise reminds me that there is a certain tragic irony in this method of avoiding conflict by silencing yourself: by removing yourself from the relationship to avoid losing said relationship you are abandoning the very thing you don't want to lose. I am left holding an empty shell. When I think back to these moments an image comes to my mind. I am holding a beautiful butterfly in the palm of my hand. As I watch the delicate and colorful wings flutter a blissful happiness suddenly morphs into an urgent fear. The butterfly could fly away at any moment. And I am struck by an urge to close my fist. To stop the butterfly from fleeing I must destroy the very thing I fear losing.

I learned from a young age that the only way to ensure people would never leave me was to become their shadow—following their footsteps and mirroring their thoughts and feelings. But it was also true that if I was a good mirror, if I had such "perfect" synchronistic relationships, it was only because there was a part of me that was not there. A part of me remained always

28

outside looking in and coordinating the action. And this part of me would be forever untouched by the joys of intimacy and the pain of its loss. A wall was set up between me and my relationships and by remaining always on the other side of that wall I abandoned every relationship before it had the potential to grow into something that could ever fall apart. The same walls that were set up to prevent people from leaving were the walls that prevented them from ever coming in.

With this early schooling in pain and loss I have become fluent in its language. I understand its movements and contours, the scars it leaves on those it touches, and can detect the footsteps of those who are running away. I heard the pitter-patter of loss as I listened to girl after girl, on the cusp of adolescence, describe her honest and authentic voice, the voice of her agency and desire, as "stupid" or "too loud." In their self-derision I could hear the voice inside my head, my repressor and protector, the voice that silences and hides me as protection from further loss. It is the voice of reason, reminding me that it is safer not to be seen or heard, to tell people the story they want to hear rather than the story I know to be true. In the decision of Iris to mute her own voice—so that she would be someone whom others wanted to be with—I could see the fingerprints of my response to my father's death, my decision to avoid further loss by taking my real feelings, needs, and desires out of my relationships. And in the voices of fathers who encouraged their sons to cover their emotional vulnerability I heard the echo of my own conviction that emotional withdrawal was the most powerful defense against abandonment—"not caring" my weapon of last resort.

Why Does Patriarchy Persist?

The voices Carol recorded in *The Birth of Pleasure* chronicled a culturally scripted journey toward feminine selflessness and masculine detachment while mine was a journey away from loss, yet the end-point was the same: away from authentic connection toward the chimera of relationship. It was easy to understand why I, in the aftermath of the death of my father, had made this painful compromise. But why in the ordinary course of development were these young girls and boys choosing to sacrifice relationship? Why was the path of development converging so precisely with a story of traumatic loss?

As I traced the connections between my personal response to trauma and the response of some boys and girls to the pressures of initiation, I began to wonder whether the forces acting on me—pressuring me to disconnect from my desire for real intimacy—were political and cultural as well as psychological. My therapist encouraged me to bring myself into relationship by seeing how my self-silencing was rooted in a fear of abandonment—a traumatic experience, linked to the death of my father, that was now far behind me. My therapist was right—my journey away from love to avoid loss could be explained by the death of my father, an understandable and common response to loss and trauma. Yet what he missed was that this journey was also culturally scripted and socially rewarded. Disconnecting parts of myself from my relationships, sacrificing authentic connection for the steady security of faux "relationships," while psychologically harmful, continued to be socially adaptive, conforming as it did to the dictates of patriarchal femininity.

30

The First Clue: An Association to Loss

Like many of the girls in Carol's studies I was doing well. I had a law degree, a boyfriend, I was forging a career in human rights. My self-contortion was socially rewarded. The barriers preventing me from bringing my real thoughts, feelings, needs, and desires into relationship were not simply psychological or rooted in a uniquely traumatic experience of loss, they were social and rooted in a culture which lauded the sacrifice of self for the sake of so-called "relationships." It suddenly became clear to me that in order to understand my own decision to separate parts of myself from my relationships—and the decisions of countless boys and girls, men and women, to do the same—we needed an explanation that was both culturally and psychologically attuned. We needed to understand the connection between the psychology of loss and the politics of patriarchy.

Could it be, I began to wonder, that my psychological response to death—the sacrifice of love to avoid further loss—highlights the psychological dynamic of a culture which forces the sacrifice of connection for the sake of hierarchy? And so it was through the lens of personal loss (loss of a father, a patriarch) that I came to question whether patriarchy has a psychological function. Within the shadows of love and intimacy lurks the threat of loss, and so, if we are afraid of love because its loss has come to feel inevitable or unbearable, patriarchy may feel like a refuge, and the journey away from love may feel like a journey toward safety.

Resistance

Carol: I remember standing in a school gymnasium with a group of eleven-year-old girls, sixth graders taking part in a week-long project to strengthen healthy resistance and courage in girls. It was June and the school was pretty much deserted, when Ted, their beloved teacher, walked into the gym and Sara, a prize-winning speed skater, shouted at him, giving voice to her anger that he was spending the week with the boys in the class and not with her. The freedom of her voice coming so directly from the very core of her being roused me like a wake-up call. I remember the sensation that passed through my body, the visceral jolt and the Proustian epiphany that followed: I know this voice. That was my voice.

A voice I knew but had forgotten. At once familiar and surprising. Like the taste of a madeleine dipped in tea, its sound opened a vast storehouse of recollection. In the after-school theater, writing and outing clubs that my colleagues and I had started, in the presence of nine-, ten-, and eleven-year-old girls, I would experience again the sensation of my voice rising from the very center of my being, free from instant second thoughts and revisions, conveying what I was feeling and thinking. I experienced it as a sensation of freedom and also as a startling reminder of how it feels to be present, to be in the moment, to be in relationship. With myself and with others. I found it exhilarating. Like speed skating.

We do not sacrifice relationship for no reason. Abraham prepares to sacrifice his son Isaac to show that he placed God above all else, Agamemnon sacrifices his

32

daughter Iphigenia to gain the winds that will carry the Greek army to Troy. There is something to be gained by the sacrifice of love, something at stake: restoring honor, proving one's devotion to God.

The sacrifice of love is the thumbprint of patriarchy. It clears the way for establishing and maintaining hierarchy. Patriarchy is an order of living that privileges some men over other men (straight over gay, rich over poor, white over black, fathers over sons, this religion over that religion, this caste over the others) and all men over women. The politics of patriarchy is the politics of domination—a politics that rationalizes inequality and turns a blind eye to what from a democratic vantage-point looks like oppression (being on the bottom, having no voice, being at the mercy of those on top). But in addition to the political forces that can explain the persistence of patriarchal institutions and values, there are also psychological forces holding these structures in place.

It is not simply that girls succumb to the pressures on them to silence an honest voice (the voice that says what they really feel and think), or that boys give into the pressures on them to cover their emotional sensitivity (their tenderness, their empathy, their vulnerability). It is not just that girls are enticed by the rewards held out to them if they turn themselves into someone others want to be with (someone who is not too loud or too angry or for that matter too honest or perceptive), or that boys can't resist the privileges offered to them in exchange for renouncing whatever is defined as feminine or maternal (having feelings, caring about people's feelings). It is also because, as Naomi points out, the sacrifice of love is a refuge against loss.

Sheila at sixteen describes this protective strategy as "brilliant." Having said that she doesn't like herself enough to look out for herself, she then says "actually"— a word I came to hear as a switch word for girls, signaling their turn from saying what they think and feel to saying what they really think and feel. So Sheila, explaining how actually she looks out for herself, says that she does so by never saying what she is feeling and thinking. That way, as she points out, it doesn't matter what people say about her since in fact they don't know who she is. "Brilliant isn't it?" she asks, and I agree. "But," I say, "it is at the expense of what you said you wanted." Sheila had said that she wanted honesty in relationships.[1]

We can understand why someone would turn away from love in the aftermath of death. But why in the so-called normal course of development or in the seeming absence of irrevocable loss or trauma would girls such as Iris and Sheila, or boys including the young boys Judy Chu followed and the adolescent boys in Niobe Way's studies, willingly forgo the pleasures of relationship, the back and forth of responsive engagement? In retrospect, the research on development shone a spotlight on why the relational play that we seek out and engage in as infants—the foundation that sets us on the path to pleasure—becomes derailed.

The psychoanalyst Adam Phillips writes: "Somewhere in ourselves we associate being loved with being betrayed and being betrayed with growing. And we do a lot of work not to know this when it is, in fact, something worth acknowledging."[2] The Oedipus myth charts this betrayal of love as well as the not knowing that follows.

Thus, it depicts the psyche's induction into patriarchy, the internalization of the masculine taboo on tenderness and the feminine taboo on having a voice of one's own. The point of initiation marks a crossroads, a turning point in development, where the betrayal of love becomes not only adaptive, the price one pays for entry into the social order (that is, for having relationships), but also seemingly inescapable: a fact worth acknowledging.

It is not altogether surprising, although it came as something of a surprise, to discover that the initiation that requires a betrayal of love is met with a healthy resistance. The commonly told story is that patriarchy persists because it gives us rewards we desire: power and privilege for those men upon whom patriarchy bestows honor, and in the case of women "honor, riches, marriage blessing"—the gifts that the goddesses in *The Tempest* bestow on Prospero's daughter Miranda.[3] This is the patriarchal explanation of patriarchy: what it bestows is what we desire. Of course we give up relationship for status and power, for material wealth and honor. Or to put it another way, it is an explanation of patriarchy which implicitly assumes a patriarchal hierarchy of values (power above people, self above relationship) as self-evident and inevitable.

But hearing Sara's voice in the gym that morning was a reminder of the price one pays. In that moment, I felt again the exquisite freedom and pleasure of being myself in relationship. Why, for all the riches in the world, would I give this up?

The healthy resistance to giving up relationship is a resistance to loss. But it is also a resistance to betraying what in truth we love, namely the pleasure of being in relationship. Adam Phillips reminds us that we have come to associate the betrayal of love with growing: with the ability to separate and stand on our own two feet, with the pride of the two year old who insists, "Me do it!"

Yet to Judy at thirteen, the resistance to losing connection is also a resistance to "forgetting your mind."[4] A participant in one of the Harvard Project studies of girls' development, Judy resists losing her mind. The mind, she explains, pointing to her gut, is "associated with your heart and your soul and your internal feeling and your real feelings."[5] She is resisting separating her mind from her brain, which she locates in her head and associates with her smartness, her intelligence, and her education. Intuitively she has come to what the neurobiologist Antonio Damasio discovered in his studies of consciousness: we register our experience in our bodies and in our emotions, picking up the music or the feeling of what happens which then plays in our minds and thoughts.[6] When we separate our minds from our bodies or, as Judy would have, it, our embodied mind from our intellectual brain, we are in danger of forgetting our mind—that is, forgetting what we know in our hearts and our souls: our internal feeling, our real feelings. And doing so in the name of smartness, intelligence, and education. In a culture that valorizes the splitting of reason from emotion, in an educational system that promotes the separation of thoughts from feelings, this move is associated with growing. Yet to Judy, it feels akin to rape: "I think that after a while, you sort of forget your mind, because everything is being shoved at you into your brain."[7]

When we forget our minds, we lose touch with ourselves, and thereby lose the capacity to be in relationship. To George, a high school junior in one of Niobe Way's studies, resistance to betraying love is a resistance not to growing but to going "wacko."[8] George says that without a best friend, without someone to tell your secrets to, you go crazy. Research backs him up.

This voice of healthy resistance was the "different voice." A key discovery of the research on development lay in the recognition that this "different" voice is a quintessentially human voice, a cadenced, relational voice. A voice that joins thought and emotion, mind with body, self with relationship. It is the voice we hear in children's emotional honesty and perceptiveness, a voice we harbor within ourselves. It only comes to sound different following an initiation that alters the resonance, changing how voices sound, and also how they are responded to and resounded by others. Thus a voice that is emotionally attuned and responsive comes to sound "feminine" and becomes associated with relationships, with caring, and with women in a society and culture where it is women who for the most part take on the responsibility of caring for others (notably for children, the old and the sick). In contrast, and in accord with the gender binary and hierarchy, a voice that is self-assertive is heard as independent and comes to sound "masculine," associated with privilege and with men in a society and culture where for the most part men hold power. In a patriarchal universe where a human voice becomes a different voice it is as though relationships and self are at opposite poles, and so after a while it becomes difficult to remember what otherwise is self-evident: that in truth, self and relationship are interdependent.

Once the gender binary governs our way of seeing and speaking, it becomes seemingly impossible to hear or lend credence to a voice that is neither selfish nor selfless, egoistic or altruistic. So powerful is the dualistic framework of the gender binary in shaping how we perceive the world, that it can literally keep us from seeing what is right in front of our eyes. It's like wearing glasses that distort perception. We lose our ability to recognize what to thirteen-year-old Judy and to sixteen-year-old George seems obvious.

The path of development then becomes a path of resistance. It begins as a healthy resistance to losing connection—the resistance we see in the protest and moves to repair made by the baby in the YouTube video. Boys do find ways to hold on to their emotional sensitivity and their desire for closeness, and girls find ways to hold on to an honest and assertive voice. But as this healthy resistance to losing relationship brings children into conflict with the gender hierarchy and binary that force the separation of thought from emotion, mind from body, and the self from relationships, and by doing so enforce a loss of relationship, the healthy resistance becomes a form of political resistance: a protest against the culture of patriarchy.

Children's healthy resistance to internalizing gendered splits and hierarchies that would lead them to forget what they know in their hearts, or to find themselves alone, at sea and in danger of going crazy, can go underground and become strategic. Neeti, an outstanding student and school leader, explains how she has preserved a voice of integrity: "The voice that stands up for what I believe in has been buried deep inside me."[9] Hidden, but not forgotten. But when the pressures of accommodation become overwhelming, when the desire to have "relationships"—to be one of the boys or a girl others want to be with—becomes too pressing or seemingly essential, political resistance can give way to what clinicians recognize as psychological resistance. That is, a political resistance can give way to repression, dissociation, and disavowal of what has come to feel too painful or shameful to hold in awareness. With this move from political to psychological resistance, the impetus to bring about change in the world is lost, and the focus turns instead to fitting oneself into the prevailing order of things.

Carrie, a participant in Lisa Machoian's 2005 study on depression in adolescent girls, chronicles this progression from a strategic resistance—whereby a girl may outwardly appear to comply with cultural conventions by carefully choosing when to speak, what to say, and when to remain silent, all the while not losing awareness of what she thinks and feels and wants to say—to a psychological resistance where internal barriers block her awareness of her feelings and keep her from knowing aspects of herself that have come to feel unseemly.[10] When Carrie speaks of being worn down by always trying to please others, she describes herself as being worn away—becoming much less of a person, becoming some other person, and by not being who she is, losing her sense of who she was. Yet at the same time, within some part of herself, Carrie knows that something is amiss because "nothing ever feels quite right":

> It really wears you down. It also wears away at you. You become so much less of a person when all you're doing is trying to please others. You are not being who you are and, after a while, you lose who you were. You become that other person. So nothing ever feels quite right, because some part of you knows that's not really you. So, you're never happy.

To recapitulate the trajectory: as a healthy resistance to losing relationship becomes a political resistance to the structures of patriarchy, it can lead to open protest, to naming the obvious and speaking truth to power. Or the resistance can go underground and become strategic. Or it can turn into a psychological resistance whereby we hold parts of our experience outside our awareness and in this way come not to know what in another part of ourselves we know. The shift into psychological resistance is when some boys begin to sound like "boys"—dismissive of or tone-deaf to their own and others' emotional needs. It is when some girls can sound like selfless good women (the mother who is always there, the daughter who is always kind, the perfect student, the always helpful colleague), disowning the voice that stands up for what they actually feel, think, desire, and believe in. With this move into psychological resistance, some boys will manifest the problems that we have come to associate with being boys (the learning and attention and speech disorders so prevalent among boys and familiar to anyone who works in schools, the out of touch or out of control behavior, and, among adolescent boys, the rise in suicide and other forms of lethal violence), and some girls will show signs of the depression, the eating disorders, the cutting, and the self-silencing that set in among girls at adolescence.

The turn from healthy protest and political resistance to psychological resistance was signaled in our interview conversations by the appearance of the injunction "Don't," an internalized prohibition that for girls came to stand between "I" and "know" and for boys between "I" and "care." This internalization of the gender binary that allocates knowing to boys and caring to girls marks an initiation whereby some girls come not to know what in fact they know and some boys not to care about both who and what in truth they care about deeply. The move from relationship into feminine self-silencing and masculine detachment—not knowing and not caring—is necessary for establishing hierarchy, which requires a loss of empathy by those on top and a loss of self-assertion by those below. Knowing and caring are integral to political resistance, and specifically to resisting the gender strictures of patriarchy that separate intelligence (knowing) from emotion (caring) and render both men and women less than fully human.

In her weekly reflection paper for the seminar on resisting injustice, Christine, a law student, writes of being challenged by her eight-year-old cousin, Akili. "Akili had asked me a question and I began my response with the refrain, 'I don't know.' She interrupted me and exclaimed: 'Stop saying I don't know'!" Christine reflects: "I hadn't even realized I'd been repeating this phrase, but Akili had noticed and wanted me to know that she trusted my capacity to speak from experience. She wanted me to be candid with her—she wanted a relationship." Christine had, in her own words, "feigned ignorance as a defense mechanism. I was protecting myself from potential conflict by hiding my potentially disruptive opinion."

Katie, a human rights lawyer studying for an advanced degree, uses the word "selfish" to explain why she is reluctant to base her research on what for her is a real question: something *she* wants to know, in contrast to something she has come to think of as worth knowing or "important."

Christine initially hides her potentially disruptive opinion to protect herself from potential conflict, until she is challenged by her eight-year-old cousin to bring herself into relationship—to speak from her experience rather than claiming not to know. Katie dismisses her question as "selfish," considering what she wants to know as not important until I, as her teacher in a seminar on listening, challenge her to listen to herself. Like Adam and Jackie, Christine and Katie are aware of the forces that lead them, as Christine says, without realizing what they are doing, to forgo relationship by holding themselves—their knowledge, their "capacity to speak from experience," and their questions—apart from their relationships and their work. In realizing what they were doing, they become aware of their complicity in the perpetuation of patriarchy—Christine to protect herself from the conflict that would potentially erupt if she were to express her potentially disruptive opinion, and Katie to avoid being "selfish." I found it telling that each of them knew precisely what was at stake.

When political resistance gave way to psychological resistance, my colleagues and I saw how it is that some women will join what can be thought of as the conspiracy of silence, whereby women do not say what they see, or know what in some part of themselves they know, just as some men will join what can best be described as the conspiracy of violence whereby they turn away from relationship, turn women into objects, and lash out when their manhood is shamed or their vulnerability exposed. Given the changes that have occurred in the lives of many women and men along with a growing awareness of the full spectrum of gender identities, the persistence of these binary codes of manhood and womanhood along with the cultures of male violence and female silence that these codes enforce and sustain becomes even more striking.

My eye was drawn to the stalwarts—those who hold to their political resistance by insisting on both having a voice and staying in relationship. Anna, fourteen and a participant in one of the studies of girls' development, exemplifies this refusal to silence her voice for the sake of "relationships" by writing two papers on the hero legend: "the one that got the A" (which as a girl from a working-class family she needed in order to win a scholarship to college) and the one she wanted to write.[11] She knew that paper would make her teacher mad because in writing what she wanted to write she was challenging her teacher's more anodyne view of the hero legend. Drawing on her experience of living with an unemployed father whose violence toward her brothers had brought social service agencies to the house, Anna saw the hero legend as dangerous, encouraging men to cover their vulnerability with violence. By turning in both papers along with a letter of explanation, Anna was risking the teacher's anger, but she was also risking relationship—that is, taking the risk that it was in fact possible for her both to have a voice of her own and to stay in relationship with her teacher. And to her credit, the teacher read both papers.

During the years I spent listening to girls and witnessing their resistance, I came to see my own experience in growing up from a new vantage-point. I understood my fights with my mother at the time of my own adolescence as not just a fight over separation (it's easier to leave when you're angry) but also a fight for something. I became aware that I had in effect two relationships with my mother: one with a woman I loved and who was herself in relationship with me, and one with a woman who appeared as the wife of my father, ensconced in being Mrs. Friedman. She was trying to warn me of what Adam the law student didn't want to look at: what would happen if he "rocked the boat." I was resisting the framework descending on me as I turned from girl to young woman, the framework of womanhood that Jackie described. It was long before I had read the myth of Psyche and Eros, but I knew I didn't want to become an object or not say or see what I knew as the price I would pay for love. I was fighting for relationship, but it was only years later, when I was studying girls and saw their resistance, that I became acutely aware of the courage we summoned and the reprisals we faced, or for that matter came to appreciate what my mother was warning me about. Like the mythic Psyche, we were courting danger, and yet also showing a surprising resilience by persevering in the face of forces that are in fact daunting.

Loss

Naomi: In retrospect it seems clear: all roads were leading us to John Bowlby and his pioneering studies of attachment and loss. At the time, it was the realization that we were dealing with forces, a system of patriarchy with its framing of manhood and womanhood, that acted on us, as Adam said, "without so much as a conscious thought." Dealing with the unconscious, we turned to psychoanalysis and specifically to the psychoanalytic literature on loss. It was Carol who in the fall of 2015 suggested that I read Freud and Melanie Klein and John Bowlby.

With Freud and Klein I ultimately hit the same roadblock. Their theories of loss tended to reify the patriarchal story: loss as inevitable and detachment as the only healthy solution—mourn the loss and then get over it or, in common parlance, "just move on." Freud describes mourning as a healthy process whereby in psychoanalytic terms the ego, the "I," detaches itself from the lost object, the one who was loved.[1] Melancholia, in contrast, is described as a pathological loss response, whereby the ongoing attachment to the lost object causes it to shadow the ego. In Freud's haunting phrase: "the shadow of the object fell upon the ego."[2]

Freud's distinction between mourning and melancholia turned on its head the picture of resistance presented by the young boys and adolescent girls. Viewed through Freud's lens, the struggle to sustain connection in the face of loss—what Carol describes as healthy resistance—appears as a pathological response to loss, a failure to mourn. Freud's understanding of healthy mourning casts boys' acceptance of their loss of close friendships as "maturing"; in the words Carol quoted from one of the boys in Niobe Way's studies, he is learning "how to be more of a man." In Freud's terms, boys have detached themselves from their lost objects—a sad but ultimately healthy move, a necessary part of growing up.

Klein's view is that the "paranoid-schizoid position" (the fear of persecution and tendency to split people into "good" and "bad") is the original position, rooted in the infant's inborn aggressive fantasies (the death instinct).[3] This view reifies Freud's interpretation of the Oedipus myth: that without civilizing influence, we are beset by destructive wishes and fantasies. Responsibility for the shattering of relationships, along with fear of others and splitting, are shifted from the culture and the parents onto the children with the result that aggression, fear of persecution, and splitting are regarded as inbuilt—the source of trauma and loss rather than their consequence. This picture of loss did not fit the research on development, which points to detachment from relationship and the splitting of people into the "good" and the "bad" (the selfless and the selfish, the emotional and the rational) as culturally mandated, precipitating a psychological crisis.

And then I read Bowlby.[4] He shifted the framework by depicting attachment as an innate human desire that persists throughout the life-cycle, and detachment—from self and from others—as a maladaptive response to the experience of lost connection. I was struck by his discovery that within all relationships are the seeds of healthy development but also of the most painful trauma. Irreparable loss of relationship, Bowlby tells us, is as painful psychologically as a severe wound is physically, and can give rise to defenses. These defenses, while protective in shielding us from relationships which have become broken beyond repair, can over time become maladaptive and destructive—cutting us off from the possibility of intimacy and connection and thus causing harm to both others and ourselves.

I felt in this insight the reverberations of Carol's discoveries. In Bowlby's observation that our capacity for relationship is our greatest source of strength and integral to our survival, I heard the echoes of Carol's recognition that boys' and girls' resistance to losing relationship is a form of healthy resistance. And in his observations that the irreparable rupturing of relationship gives way to the defensive disconnection from relationship and also from parts of ourselves, I detected the markings of Carol's observation that when the pressures of accommodation become too much, a healthy resistance can give way to a form of psychological resistance—a disconnection from self and others that feels at the time protective. Delving into Bowlby's discoveries further illuminated the psychological forces driving this move from healthy to psychological resistance.

Observing the responses of young children to separations from their caregivers led Bowlby to lay out three stages of loss response: protest, despair, and detachment.[5] In subsequent work he observed that detachment takes two forms: compliant relatedness (termed by Bowlby anxious attachment/compulsive caregiving), or relational avoidance and emotional detachment (labelled avoidant attachment/compulsive self-reliance).

Protest
Reading Bowlby's descriptions of children's protest responses[6]—clinging, crying, calling, and attempts to search for the caregiver—I was impressed by how closely these protests against loss parallel, albeit at an earlier stage of development, Carol, Chu, and Way's descriptions of girls' and boys' "healthy resistance" to an initiation that would force a loss of relationship— a loss otherwise deemed a move toward masculine independence or feminine selflessness and considered a normal part of growing up. A touching and illuminating example of protest is Bowlby's description of two-year-old Laura, who, some months after her return from an eight-day separation from her mother during a stay in hospital, looked reproachfully at her mother and demanded "Where was you, Mummy? Where was you?"[7] In Laura's protest, I hear the echoes of Sara, the prize-winning speed skater's protest against her teacher's absence, her anger at his spending the week with the boys and not with her and the other girls in the class. "Where were you Ted?" she was in effect asking him.

Listening to the angry demands and desperate cries of children like Laura led Bowlby to what at the time was a radical discovery: protest against loss is not a sign of emotional immaturity or psychological weakness (which was the commonly held view), but an in-built and healthy response to the sadness of losing touch, a response designed to restore connection with the caregiver, and thus integral to the child's survival. Bowlby's discovery mirrors what the girls and boys in Carol and Way's studies knew intuitively—their resistance was not to growing, but to losing what they recognized as a vital connection (with their own internal feelings and with other people). Moreover, what was so striking to me was Bowlby's observation that this response arises in reaction to both physical separation and emotional mis-attunement.[8] Thus our need for "attachment" speaks to the importance of emotional connection as well as physical security. Bowlby's concept of attachment thus mirrors Carol's definition of relationship as an experience of living in connection. His finding that children will protest the loss of emotional presence thus echoes Carol's finding that children will resist the sacrifice of relationship for the set and scripted "relationships" of patriarchy.

Moreover, Bowlby's observation that protest is a response to both physical separation and emotional mis-attunement suggests that children have the capacity to pick up and resist a whole range of relational violations, from the most overt forms of abuse or injustice to the subtlest experiences of disconnection or mis-attunement. Children will thus attempt to ensure that even the most asymmetrical of relationships, in the sense of there being an imbalance of ability and power (for example, that of mother and child), are responsive to the needs of the most vulnerable. From this perspective the child–parent relationship sets a template for a more nuanced understanding of the difference between hierarchy and equality, authoritarianism and democracy, an understanding based on the level of responsiveness and presence rather than sameness of treatment.[9]

There is something radical and largely overlooked in Bowlby's observations of an initial protest phase. It challenges the commonly held view that our personalities and modes of relating are shaped purely by the distinctive cultural or family environments we find ourselves born into. It shows instead that there is an element of agency from the beginning and that with this we have the capacity to resist external influence and to mold our relationships so they better fit our idiosyncratic needs and desires. I find this particularly significant and hopeful in terms of our thinking about why patriarchy persists. For it suggests that within each of us are the seeds of resistance—the ability to challenge cultural prescriptions that are inimical to our most basic relational desires and needs. This is not just some abstract hope—it was the protesting cries of children against the lack of emotional attention and contact with caregivers in institutional settings that led Bowlby to push for and achieve radical reform of these practices.[10]

Despair
Bowlby observed that when protest fails to bring about reconnection, it gives way to despair: the giving up of hope that what has been lost can be found. During this phase the child makes no overt moves toward reconnection. Bowlby notes that this emotional withdrawal

is a mark of psychological distress, rather than a sign of recovery as it was commonly mistaken for.[11]

In following the path from protest to despair, Bowlby observed the shifting tides of anger.[12] Accompanying the protest phase, he noted a functional anger—"the anger of hope" that serves to mobilize the child's efforts to re-establish contact with his or her caregiver. Bowlby stressed that this anger—often expressed as reproachful and punishing behavior—"acts to promote, and not to disrupt, the bond."[13] However, when protest fails to effect reconnection, this anger of hope gives way to a dysfunctional anger—"the anger of despair": a "deep-running resentment" leading to the cold "malice of hatred."[14] This anger laced with resentment and hatred becomes a threat to relationship and so tends not to be expressed directly against the person responsible for the loss, but to be repressed, redirected against the self or projected onto others—typically someone weaker.[15] In this way the child defends against loss by accepting the relational violation, either turning the anger back on the self or becoming the aggressor and inflicting losses on others. Silence and violence thus mark the shift from protest to despair.

The despair phase is a quiet stage of inactivity, characterized by the absence of a resisting voice. We see the helplessness and lethargy associated with depression along with the loss of pleasure and change in voice that signal the loss of connection. The signs of psychological distress that rise among boys between ages four and seven, among girls between eleven and fourteen, and then boys during mid to late adolescence can be recognized as manifestations of the despair that Bowlby observed among children when their protests against loss proved ineffective. Viewed in this light, these signs of psychological distress reflect the sense of futility and loss of trust that arise when attempts to repair ruptures in relationship fail. Their increase at these times of initiation suggest the toll that the induction into the gender codes of patriarchy takes on the psyche. The loss of connection is reflected in the shift from the "anger of hope" to the "anger of despair"—a shift that occurs when trust that the loss can be repaired is shattered.

With Bowlby's observation that where pleas are made in vain, a child learns that the effort to effect change is unavailing and so gives up, I began to think about how the pressures placed on boys to become "brave boys"—and not express their tenderness and their need for care—and on girls to become "good girls"—and not express their desires or agency or be angry on their own behalf—undermine their ability to effectively protest breaks in connection and can lead them to give up, to shift from protesting to acquiescing in the loss of relationship.

Detachment

The aspect of Bowlby's work which proved most enlightening was his observation that when connection is still not restored, despair gives way to detachment. Detachment is a dissociative defense that seeks to eliminate the potential for irreparable rupture by splitting parts of the self, notably the longing for relationship, off from awareness. In the clinical literature, psychoanalyst Susan Sands writes, "Dissociative defenses serve to regulate relatedness to others ... The dissociated patient is attempting to stay enough in relationship with the human environment to survive the present while, at the same time, keeping the needs for more intimate relatedness sequestered but alive."[16] These observations set the stage for a deeper understanding of the external pressures and psychological dynamics that trigger the move from healthy resistance to psychological resistance and with it the sacrifice of relationship for "relationships."

In the detachment phase, Bowlby notes, a child will "act as if neither mothering nor contact with humans has much significance for him" and "he will become increasingly self-centered and, instead of directing his desires and feelings towards people, will become preoccupied with material things."[17] The child will "appear cheerful and adapted to his unusual situation and apparently easy and unafraid of anyone. But this sociability is superficial; he *appears* no longer to care for anyone."[18] Once detachment sets in, we disavow and disconnect from our need for care and human connection, and as we turn away from relationship we can compensate for the loss by becoming increasingly self-centered and more concerned with objects than with people—a strategy Bowlby termed "compulsive self-reliance."[19]

Bowlby's understanding of detachment essentially flips Freud's distinction between healthy mourning and pathological melancholia on its head. It is the detached person for whom the lost object along with the desire for relationship become shadows that fall upon the psyche. Meaning the detached person holds on to their desire for love and the pain of loss, but relegates these feelings to their unconscious, so they become a sort of haunting, casting a ghost-like shadow over their ability to form relationships.

Listening closely to the words of young children separated from their caregivers, and observing their expressions, affect, and gestures, had alerted Bowlby to an internal struggle for connection in these apparently self-sufficient children—a struggle that had not been seen before. This struggle undermined the prevailing wisdom that detachment is a healthy response to loss and a sign of recovery as well as a move toward greater independence and maturity. In a particularly illuminating instance Bowlby describes two-and-a-half-year-old Kate, who, during her second week of separation from her mother, began to seem preoccupied and dreamy and on one occasion queried, "What is Kate looking for?"[20] Bowlby takes this question seriously, not as a sign of cognitive confusion or developmental retardation, but rather to indicate that she, Kate, was beginning to detach herself from her yearning and searching for her mother by disconnecting from herself. There is someone (Kate) who is looking for something, but she (the speaker) is no longer sure who or what Kate is looking for.

This description is moving and Bowlby's interpretation compelling. He sees that when protest is thwarted or fails to bring about reconnection we lose trust in the reliability and reparability of human connection. Relational yearning continues, but is experienced as a prelude to loss and betrayal. Close observation led Bowlby to stress that when children act as if they no longer care it is not a sign that they have stopped longing for love. It's a demonstration that hopeless longing has become too painful to pursue. Then any emotion, thought, image, or memory that might remind them of their desire for love and connection, and of the fact that this desire has not been met, becomes excluded from conscious awareness in a defense that Bowlby labels "deactivation."[21]

This understanding of what lies behind detachment informs Anna Deveare Smith's play *Notes from the Field*, which among other things takes on the school-to-prison pipeline. Commenting on the practice of ejecting from school those children who by their attitudes and actions push everyone away, a teacher says that the response to such children should be "Closer, not further." By drawing them closer rather than pushing them further away, she would address the underlying issue, by conveying to these children that their longing for love is not in fact hopeless.[22]

In a 1979 paper entitled "On Knowing What You Are Not Supposed to Know and Feeling What You Are Not Supposed to Feel,"[23] Bowlby describes how in environments where children are pushed away and pressured not to express—or even feel—distress following separation, they will "shut away all the feeling they have about their loss."[24] Detachment thus takes two forms: an external disconnection from others, which is driven by an internal disconnection from the full spectrum of emotions.

Bowlby's observation that detachment can be mistaken for independence and maturity led me to an epiphany: detachment is mistaken for maturity precisely because it mirrors the pseudo-independence of manhood, which in patriarchy is synonymous with being fully human. It is striking how closely Bowlby's description of detachment tracks cultural ideals of masculine autonomy and captures the familiar persona of the emotionally stoic man more concerned with the accumulation of power and the provision of material security than with emotional intimacy or human connection.

Once I recognized this connection I couldn't read Chu and Way's descriptions of boys' becoming "boys" and men without hearing the echoes of Bowlby's descriptions of detached children. For example, Fernando, as a sensitive and chubby-cheeked fourteen year old, names friendship and education among his "most important" values: "Education's important cause I want to be somebody someday and having a lot of friends is important, that way I won't be by myself, or you know, just be lonely."[25] However by his sophomore year Fernando has shifted his focus from becoming somebody and having a lot of friends to the accumulation of possessions, girls as well as clothes and money: "I matured a lot [since last year]. More into girls, clothes. That's basically my environment and my world. Clothes, girls, and money."[26] Embracing the equation of maturity and masculinity with being independent and affluent, Fernando states that the most important things for him this year are "Sports ... me being a guy of course, I mean I love sports ... girls ... and money's important too because I mean I want to look hot ... and I could buy my mum some diamond earrings or whatever."[27]

Like many of the boys in Way's studies, Fernando attributes this shift to maturity. Yet, in fleeting moments of vulnerability, he reveals a deeper story. He describes an ongoing desire for connection, which has come under threat and so needs to be held at bay due to an increasing loss of trust in his friendships and a fear of betrayal. When asked, at fourteen, to describe his best friendship Fernando says "I can't explain it. I don't know why ... like he trusts me and I trust him."[28] By sophomore year this trust is under siege. When describing his friend Santiago he says "he trusts me with a lot of things, a lot of secrets. So if he can open up to me, once again, I think I should probably do the same. But with my close friends, I don't know, they have like two sides to them sometimes. Like Marcelo, he acts real cool with you and then, I don't know, he's kinda sneaky. So I gotta keep my eye on him."[29] In other rare moments, expressions of emotional desire emerge but are quickly covered over—or negated—with assertions of masculinity. Asked, on his final interview, about ideal friendship he says "Um, you gotta, I guess just be there for me? I guess, I don't wanna sound too sissy-like."[30] Fernando reveals a central conflict for boys during late adolescence: he wants a close connection but worries that if he expresses this desire betrayal will ensue as he will be labelled a sissy—either way the loss of connection is seemingly inevitable. Thus, as Way points out, Fernando's increasing lack of intimacy does not come from a lack of desire, but from a lack of trust that his secrets will be kept confidential[31] and, I would add, that expressions of vulnerability will not be laughed at or ridiculed.

As with detached children who in response to irreparable loss turn their attention away from their caregivers to the presents that they provide, Fernando's shift away from friendships to possessions can be seen as a form of sublimation, whereby an unacceptable and increasingly risky and seemingly futile desire for connection is transformed into an acceptable desire for the things that will make him "look hot." It is not simply that these "things" (sports, girls, money) are more acceptable, but, having lost trust in human connection, these objects (or people turned into objects), being more subject to our control, have come to seem more reliable than the relationships they have replaced. Thus, replacing a desire for relationship with a desire for accumulation can signify, in Fernando's words, "being a guy," but this construction of masculinity as self-sufficiency can also reflect an effort to quell a fear of inadequacy and avoid the potential for rupture or betrayal.[32] This suggests that what has been taken as natural—a guy's privileging of things over people—is a material solution to a feeling of insufficiency and a means of compensating for the experience of losing trust in the reliability of relationship. The objectification of women and the investment in things also become face-saving mechanisms, whereby a guy can surreptitiously satisfy his "feminine" desires. Materialism becomes a cover, a defense against just being lonely. Fernando thus alerts us to the potential that any threat to a guy's status or wealth—or to his possession of women—can trigger a painful yet incommunicable sense of loneliness and loss, that for the sake of manhood will have to be covered.

In this way, Bowlby's work on loss and attachment illuminates the psychological function that patriarchal masculinity can serve. It shows detachment to be both a symptom of a past loss and a defense against the pain of future loss in the same way that a scab is a sign of a physical wound and a defense against further pain and injury. When we cut through our skin's surface a protective crust forms, preventing further infection and allowing the wound to heal. In the same way, when an experience of rupture cuts through a relationship, a protective layer is built internally between ourselves and our most vulnerable feelings and externally between ourselves and other people.

In adverse environments, this protective layer can serve a psychologically adaptive and protective function. In environments which are unresponsive to, or critical of, a child's expression of their desire for love and need for support, as patriarchy is for boys, the child can learn to minimize expression of these needs to avoid further rejection. It is as if the individual thinks "if I never allow myself to hope for a good relationship, then I will never again feel the pain of despair should that hope be dashed." Or in the words of Tyrone—a participant in Way's study—"I don't want to get too close to anybody cause I don't want to lose them."[33] To avoid the pain of further loss, children raised in environments of emotional scarcity or adversity may sacrifice the hope or deny the very possibility of love. Shawn, one of the boys in Way's studies, at the age of eighteen makes this defensive logic explicit: he would rather live alone and unknown behind an impenetrable wall than risk being open and thereby vulnerable to being broken apart by people:

I've got like a brick wall around me ... gonna take a lot just to get inside me ... 'cause I see many people out

here, they be open [with each other] and many people
could find a way to break them apart. But I don't want
nobody knowing me and being able to break me apart
and do anything they want with me.[34]

For boys like Shawn who have come to fear that
to be open and vulnerable is to be broken apart,
manhood—or more precisely the pseudo-independence
and emotional detachment that pass for manhood in
their evocation of superiority and strength—becomes a
refuge and a solace.

However, by disconnecting from other people
and shielding themselves from the emotional world
around them, detached individuals, trapped in a barren
emotional landscape, by their very detachment inflict
on others the experiences of neglect and rejection they
themselves had set out to shield themselves against.
Thus the detachment defense can set into motion a
vicious cycle of loss, especially since when the defense
breaks down, anger, hostility, and violence (against self
and/or others) can erupt in an effort to keep the pain of
the loss from breaking through.

It is in the work of psychiatrist James Gilligan and
his theorizing on the causes and prevention of violence
that we see most deeply into these links between loss
and shame and manhood and violence.[35] In his work
with violent men in jails and prisons and his treatment
of the criminally insane, he not only witnessed extremes
of detachment but also saw how the detachment and
cruelty of these men reflected their own extreme experiences of trauma and of neglect—an absence of love so
daunting as to at times strain credulity. The detachment

defense was prominent in these men and their violence often served as a cover, an attempt to protect themselves from feelings of need and longings to be cared for. These feelings were so painful and shameful and consequently so well hidden that only the most discerning eye could detect how the violent act itself, while affirming a man's masculinity and covering his reawakened longing, can also serve as the means for him to ensure that by going to prison he will at last be cared for. In this way, violent men may provide the starkest glimpse into the heart of darkness at the core of patriarchal masculinity.

In subsequent work, Bowlby found that that the detachment defense can take an inverse form, which he described as anxious attachment.[36] Rather than avoiding or detaching from relationships, the anxiously attached cling to others, often with excessive submissiveness and engaging in what Bowlby termed "compulsive caregiving" as a substitute for actual relationship.[37] Anxious attachment as a form of "compliant relatedness"[38] is characterized by a restriction of initiative and a ban on freedom of expression. Compulsive caregiving is a form of vicarious caring whereby the compulsive caregiver seems to be attributing to the "cared-for all the sadness and neediness that he is unable or unwilling to recognize in himself."[39] This form of relating reflects an under-lying conviction that the loved one will not be available (meaning responsive and accessible) unless one hovers close and tries to please. Still hoping for love and care and yet deeply anxious lest they be neglected or rejected, the anxiously attached cling to the other, forming symbiotic "relationships" (relationships where two people function as one) by in effect submerging themselves in the other.

In order to achieve this seemingly protective state of oneness, anxiously attached children compromise their autonomy, their desire to play and to explore, alongside any independent thoughts and feelings. Knowledge and desires which have been treated as impermissible and feelings which have been received as dangerous come to be shielded not simply from the world but also from their own conscious awareness. Bowlby describes this intrapsychic defense mechanism as "cognitive discon-nection."[40] The person literally disconnects their feelings from their thoughts and in this way feelings of hurt and anger become split off from conscious awareness of what caused this emotional response. This enables the person to interpret experiences of rupture, neglect, or mis-attunement as a sign of their own deficiency, helplessness, or unlovability, and to redirect the anger and blame back at themselves (or at weaker others).

Women who come not to know what they know and to form "perfect" relationships, meaning relationships without conflict or freedom of expression, resemble anxiously attached children. As the psychologist Dana Jack points out, this parallel suggests that "like an insurance policy, designed to protect against the possibility of loss, compliance in relationship is one way a woman attempts to guarantee that her partner will be 'accessible and potentially responsive' in times of need."[41] It's as if the woman thinks if I become who the other person wants me to be I can avoid rejection or ensure protection; or, as Sheila points out, if I am rejected, it doesn't really matter because it is not my actual self who is being rejected. Merging with the other, becoming literally selfless, is a strategy to avoid rejection, but one that comes at the cost of genuine intimacy—of relationship. By disconnecting from herself, the selfless woman renders the give and take of love outside the realm of possibility. Thus anxious attachment, like patriarchal femininity, gives rise to a form of pseudo-relationality.

I began to wonder whether Bowlby's description of anxious attachment and the defense mechanisms underlying it could shed light on how and why some of the girls in Carol's studies came literally not to know what on some level they knew. Just as the "I don't care" that rose in frequency among the boys in Way's studies signals the deactivation defense whereby detached children disconnect from their relational desires and capacities, so the "I don't know" that became the marker of some girls' entry into young womanhood signals the cognitive disconnection whereby children come not to know why they feel what they feel. In this way both the anxiously attached children observed by Bowlby and the girls in Carol's studies shut out knowledge and feelings that others don't want them to have—knowledge which they fear has the power to destroy their relationships irreparably.

The brilliance of cognitive disconnection as a defense against an actual or threatened loss is that we are able to build an illusory image of the caregiver and of our relationships as all good (and of ourselves as lacking). This operates as a buffer against the more painful—and disruptive—knowledge that the other has been careless with us and our relationships lacking.[42] In the poignant words of psychoanalyst R. W Fairbairn, "it is better to be a sinner in a world ruled by God than to live in a world ruled by the devil."[43]

Bowlby challenged the commonly held view that young children, being totally dependent on their parents' care, are strongly biased to see them in a favorable light and so to exclude contrary information. Instead he observed that children only come to negate their own perceptions in environments where "on threat of not being loved or even of being abandoned a child is led to understand that he is not supposed to notice his parents' adverse treatment of him or, if he does, that he should regard it as being no more than the justifiable reaction of a wronged parent to his (the child's) bad behaviour."[44]

Reading this I think of the pressure placed on girls at the cusp of womanhood not to know what they know. According to Bowlby's model, our first response to relational injustice or betrayal is not distortion and compliance, but protest. It is only when our protest is futile, when seeing and complaining are punished or lead nowhere, that we come to distort our narrative—to see the world as fair and any adverse treatment our just desert.

The footprints of cognitive disconnection are discernable in the ways we have neutralized the force of patriarchy in our lives. For a woman, however, the relinquishing of her own perspective—or perhaps better to say, the impermissibility of her having a voice of her own—is built into the very notion of what it means to be a "good woman." The relational merger and concurrent loss of independence and autonomy that Bowlby observed in anxiously attached children have been celebrated as the hallmarks of feminine goodness. To bring her own voice or assert her own perspective in relationships, meaning for her to be truly in relationship—that is, to do something that seems natural and good—becomes under patriarchy a bad, selfish, and dangerous act. As with the children Bowlby studied, the pressures placed on women to see the world as fair, to not notice adverse treatment, or to see such treatment as a just desert, a justifiable response to their behavior, are all too real. Specifically, like the anxiously attached children, it is on threat of not being loved or even of being abandoned that some girls come not to know what they know.

It comes as something of a surprise to recognize that we are still dealing with this. The persistence of patriarchy in the voice of a millennial woman is unexpected. It takes a moment to register the word "selfish" in listening to the successful bi-racial (Anglo-Asian) human rights lawyer who has enrolled in Carol's research seminar, who is now pursuing an advanced law degree and yet speaks of her reluctance to base her research on her own question because to do so would be "selfish," just "something I want to know" rather than something "important."

How close she comes, I find myself thinking, though the thought itself feels forbidden, to Woolf's description of the Angel in the House, the nineteenth-century icon of feminine goodness who "never had a mind or wish of her own, but preferred to sympathize always with the minds and wishes of others."[45] Woolf wrote these words in her 1931 essay "Professions for Women," recognizing that even more pernicious perhaps than formal restrictions on women's access to higher education or professional opportunities are the cultural expectations that would block a woman from having access to her own mind. Thanks to the efforts of pioneers such as Woolf, I (along with many other women of my generation) have benefitted from the educational and financial opportunities denied to all women in previous generations. We in the colleges and professions that Woolf advocated for women to enter are often explicitly encouraged to speak out, and sometimes even rewarded for it. However, at the same time, expressing certain thoughts and feelings, our needs, our desires, or god forbid our dissatisfaction, frustration, or anger, continues to be a "risky" business. We risk being labelled "shrill," "too emotional," irrational, stupid, and ridiculed for not being able to take a joke, accused of ruining men's fun, their reputations, their lives. At worst, we face violent reprisals. Reprisals which are then justified as legitimate responses to our failure to charm, or for our being too aggressive, too sexual, too much. Reprisals which we are paradoxically told we could have avoided if only we had been more assertive, as if knowing and protesting were not the very acts that imperil our relationships and thus, if not our survival, our chances for advancement. The contradiction is astounding: a woman is blamed for simultaneously being too assertive (too demanding, too aggressive, in a word, selfish) and not assertive enough (why didn't you walk away or fight back, she is told). Both reinforce the illusion that the world is fair, patriarchy is a thing of the past, and it is individuals who are lacking. This is precisely the dynamic, the blaming of individuals for systemic injustice, that led three radical black women organizers to initiate the Black Lives Matter movement.

The brake on exploration and the sacrifice of a mind of one's own for the sake of so-called "relationships" continue in spite of all the changes that have occurred in many women's lives. Selflessness is still regarded by many as the sine qua non of feminine goodness—the antithesis of a scarlet letter. Today's "Angel" is no longer restricted to being in the house. She may have escaped the enforced domesticity which shackled her Victorian counterpart, yet the expectations of selflessness and self-sacrificial caregiving have followed her into the workplace, into the boardroom, and into the halls of politics. And, to borrow Woolf's words, the expectation that women "charm, they must conciliate, they must—to put it bluntly—tell lies if they are to succeed,"[46] continues to constrain a woman's ability to say what she really thinks and feels and knows, and thus to effect change in these realms which some women are now privileged to enter.

The so-called inversion of caregiving roles that Bowlby observed in compulsively caregiving children, where one conceals one's desire and need for care by caring compulsively for others (as a mode of displacement but also in the hope that they may get the hint), is a socially scripted transition, experienced by girls when they feel pressed to become "good" women, first at the cusp of adolescence, and then for some when they transition to becoming mothers. But the maternal ideal also constrains women who don't become mothers. The icon of the all-giving mother creates the expectation that all women will selflessly help others, be they family members, colleagues, customers, clients, employers, and so forth. Caretakers hired to look after the children of others or take care of their elders, like many who work in the helping professions, are expected to work for low wages on the assumption that goodness is its own reward and that the one who cares needs no further compensation.

Bowlby's observation that compulsive caregiving is pathological because it creates a barrier to receiving the love and care that we all desire and need[47] echoes Carol's observation that the feminine imperative to care selflessly for others acts as a barrier to relationship, since it forces the woman to absent herself. The equation of caring with selflessness is a powerful obstacle to women having a voice, and thus to having their experience—their thoughts, their feelings, their desires and beliefs—taken into consideration. By holding up the selfless carer as a feminine icon or ideal, the culture of patriarchy encourages a woman's defensive sacrifice of relationship for "relationships." At the same time, it masks the activity that caring entails along with the sheer impossibility of caring for someone without being present and in relationship with the person or persons being cared for. By masking the intelligence and the abilities that go into caring, it also justifies paying carers low wages.

In the months of working on this project I have become attuned to a narrative which runs through countless conversations with friends about romantic relationships—bright and successful women who lament the way so much of their personality and habits change in these relationships with men. The women come to question who they really are, and then, being straight women, long for a man who by seeing them and loving them will affirm and help them rediscover the sense of self they find themselves relinquishing. I wish this were a narrative I didn't so often find myself repeating. I have come to reflect on all the various ways in which I and other millennial women—whether explicitly or implicitly—have been told and continue to be told that by meeting the needs of others in a way that negates our own needs, we will have our needs met by them, and that the sense of self we have compromised in order to have these "relationships" can be rediscovered through the love and recognition of a more powerful other.

I can't believe I am repeating this patriarchal script. Despite the many substantial gains made by professional women such as myself and the many successes of feminism, the shaming of a woman's honest voice as "selfish," self-absorbed, too loud, too much, and the continuing idealization of selflessness among women, however disguised, create a situation of forced defensiveness. The desire for relationship continues to be sacrificed for the sake of having "relationships," in the hope that perhaps in this way desires and needs and perspectives that cannot be voiced will somehow be satisfied. This patriarchal script operates according to the same vicarious model that Bowlby observed in compulsive caregivers. Just as Bowlby saw that the cared-for person comes to stand vicariously for the one giving the care, women are still told, albeit in more subtle ways, that the pleasures they deny themselves can be experienced vicariously through their spouse and/or children, or the other people and causes to which they "selflessly" commit.

This brings us to a larger and more significant observation. Attachment theorists have observed that the two defenses against loss—anxious attachment or compulsive caregiving, and avoidant attachment or compulsive self-reliance—can work in tandem to create systems of mutual projection; for example, in peer groups avoidants tend to be bullies and the anxiously attached their victims. Each projects onto the other the disowned part of his or her self, which they envy and cannot relinquish. The bullies project onto their victims the vulnerability, desire for recognition, and sadness they dare not admit, while the victims project onto the bullies the assertiveness and power they dare not claim as their own.[48] Relationships of mutuality—the cornerstone of intimacy—are thus exchanged for relationships of complementarity, relationships where each person unconsciously seeks to find in the other the thing they cannot admit to or accept in themselves.

I was struck by the way in which patriarchy—a heteronormative culture based on the supposed complementarity of men and women—rests on just such a system of mutual projection. Pressure is exerted on women to become the container into which men can project their disavowed emotions and need for care as well as their vulnerability. In order to remain the container for men's vulnerability and dependence, women must relinquish their capacity to take care of themselves. And the idea of the powerful, invulnerable man becomes the container into which a woman can pour all the desires and capacities that she has been pressed to disavow. This explains why any resistance or refusal on the part of a man or a woman to be these containers, or for that matter to fit themselves into the gender binary, triggers a backlash, the force of which continues to take us by surprise.

Writing this I think of how within a patriarchal culture every step toward women's liberation can be experienced by men as a threat of loss. So long as women assume the position of selfless caregiver—meeting men's needs for care while concealing what they are doing and thus maintaining the fiction that these needs do not exist—men do not have to reckon with their longing for care, since it is only when a need is not met that we become fully aware of it. Women's moves toward freedom can thus reawaken feelings men have experienced as shameful—desires for love and tender compassion that they have had to conceal in becoming men. In this light, the violence and the backlash against feminism can be seen not only to reflect men's fears that if women are liberated men will lose status and power or their honor; they may also reveal how women have served as the containers and concealers of needs that men have felt forced to disavow. In this sense violence or the threat of violence becomes a way to dispel shameful feelings of vulnerability and longing, and also a desperate attempt to keep women from leaving. For a woman in an abusive relationship with a man, her most dangerous move, the move that places her in greatest danger, is her move to leave him.

In summary, Bowlby's work shows that the experience of despair—the loss of trust in the possibility of relationship following an experience of separation—can lead to two defensive patterns: symbiosis-like attachment and detachment from relationship, what we have called pseudo-relationships and pseudo-independence. These defensive styles of relating, moving from the fused and enmeshed to the distant and detached, are ultimately concerned with defending against the same unbearable threat of irreparable loss. Both defenses rest on the sacrifice of authentic connection as protection against the pain of a loss that has come to seem inescapable. Hence the willingness to give up relationship for "relationships." Hence the connection between the psychology of loss and the persistence of patriarchy.

With this in mind, we come to our three discoveries.

The Three Discoveries

Carol: Our first discovery followed from the observation that the trajectory of resistance that my colleagues and I had witnessed in our studies of development parallels the trajectory of responses to loss that Bowlby describes. The move from a healthy resistance to political resistance to psychological resistance or dissociation tracks the move from protest to despair and detachment. The conclusion seemed obvious: the initiation into patriarchy entails a confrontation with loss. What's more, we had observed the loss: the sacrifice of relationship in order to have "relationships." It was the price of acceptance into a patriarchal order.

The mechanism also seemed clear. The gender binary, by splitting reason (masculine), along with mind and thought, from emotion and feelings (feminine), interrupts what Damasio, LeDoux, and other neuroscientists have shown to be the vital connections between our thoughts and our emotions—connections that, in the absence of trauma, are neurologically set.[1] It is trauma, not development, that separates reason from emotion, as Damasio explains in his book *Descartes' Error*. What had been taken as the sine qua non of rationality (reason unsullied by emotion), was revealed instead to be a manifestation of injury.

Similarly with the splitting of the self (masculine) from relationships (feminine). With the desire and ability to engage responsively with others evident, at least in rudimentary form, practically from birth, the separation of the self from relationships, once seen as the marker of autonomy and emotional maturity, suggests an encounter with traumatic loss. The confirmation of this suspicion is the radical contribution of Bowlby's work.

As in tellings of the Oedipus myth that neglect to mention its origins in trauma, prior to these advances in neuroscience and attachment theory, trauma had masqueraded as nature or been mistaken for development. Thus patriarchy with its gender binary and hierarchy was considered to be part of the natural order of things, until the studies of girls' development shone a spotlight on girls' resistance. What previously had been described as girls' problems with separation appeared, upon closer inspection, to be a problem girls were having with a patriarchal culture that was forcing them to silence an honest voice as the price for having "relationships." The studies with girls exposed a psychological incoherence at the core of what had passed for psychological development—the choice between having a voice (a self) or having relationships made no sense.

What's more, the more savvy and shrewd girls in the studies named it. When Noura, aged thirteen, describes a "perfect relationship" as one where you "never have any fights ... Like never arguing, like 'oh yeah, I totally agree with you',"[2] you know she is speaking tongue in cheek.

As it turns out this is no secret. In the name of caring about other people's feelings, for the sake of getting along and not rocking the boat, or creating conflict or appearing selfish and coming across as rude and unpleasant, girls becoming women are encouraged not to argue, not to fight but to "totally agree." In a myriad of ways, more or less subtle, they are told to take themselves (their honest voice, the voice that gives expression to their internal feelings, their real feelings, the voice that says what they "actually" think and feel or want and know) out of their relationships, and in exchange for this silencing of self and sacrifice of relationship, blessings are bestowed: honor, riches, marriage (as the goddesses promise Miranda in *The Tempest*), jobs, scholarships, the list is endless. But this too was no secret. As Emily Dickinson had written, "Ourself behind ourself, concealed / Should startle most."[3] In her diary, Anne Frank confessed, "I have, as it were, a dual personality," and then added, further down in the same entry, "I never utter my real feelings about anything."[4]

The spotlight on girls made it easier to recognize in boys a similarly strategic withdrawal from relationships—the shielding of their emotional sensibilities and intelligence that Judy Chu picked up, and the backing away from close friendships with other boys,

the friendships in which they share deep secrets, that
Niobe Way captured by asking boys about their friendships. The deep secret was really no secret. All you had
to do was ask and then listen with an ear also tuned for
what was not being said and for the cultural framework
that was keeping us from seeing what was right in front
of our eyes, or hearing what it took only a question or
two and a receptive presence to call forth—that is, from
knowing what in another sense was obvious.

And yet, even now, writing this, I feel a certain
reluctance to talk about patriarchy. As if somehow it is
shameful to name it. Or perhaps because to talk about
patriarchy is to walk into a swamp of misinterpretation.

In this respect, the discovery was clarifying. Children's
resistance to an initiation driven by a gender binary and
hierarchy (the building blocks of a patriarchal order)
follows the same trajectory as children's responses to
loss: protest, followed by despair and detachment.
The significance of patriarchy is its investment in the
move from protest to detachment; that is, in the loss
of relationship—the betrayal of love or the silencing
of self—which removes a major obstacle to the preservation (across generations) of hierarchy.

To put it very concretely: when a boy cries and is
then laughed at or shunned, or when a girl says what
she actually feels and thinks and is then excluded, their
encounter with the codes and scripts of patriarchal
manhood and womanhood registers as a rupture of
relationship. If you look closely at children when this
happens, you will see the loss of pleasure and hear the
change in their voice. Following enough such encounters,
once their initiation is complete, any move toward

relationship will place their manhood or womanhood on the line.

This loss of relationship has been rationalized, justified as a necessary sacrifice or a cost of growing up. It has been spoken of as a move from dependence to independence, from rudeness to politeness and consideration. But these moves to comply with the gender codes of patriarchy are met with resistance because with the compromise of our relational intelligence we lose the relationships that we actually need and want, relationships which have now been shown in a myriad of studies to be associated with health, longevity, and even the absence of math anxiety.[5]

A healthy resistance to losing connection, however, brings children into conflict with the forces invested in boys' willingness to sacrifice relationships and girls becoming compliant or selfless. The protest of a healthy resistance then turns into the protest of a political resistance, which in the absence of resonance or in the face of threat or danger comes under pressure to become a psychological resistance, that is, a reluctance to know what one knows, which then paves the way for the move from despair to detachment.

In this light the sudden heightened incidence of signs of psychological distress among boys between the ages of four and seven, girls roughly between eleven and fourteen, and boys in mid to late adolescence makes sense. It is consonant with the view that these are times of an initiation driven by gender that places children psychologically at risk because of the threat to relationship. The signs or symptoms are familiar to anyone who lives or works with children: the flattening of emotional responsiveness in some boys around the ages of six and seven along with the sudden high incidence around this time of learning and attention and speech disorders, the fact that depression is more common in boys than in girls up until adolescence, and then at adolescence the sudden high rates of depression among girls along with the eating disorders, the cutting and other forms of destructive behavior, and among boys in mid to late adolescence the rising rates of suicide and other forms of lethal behavior. These signs and symptoms of psychological distress can be seen as indices of the despair and detachment that Bowlby observed among children when their protests against loss proved ineffective.

Discovery #2: The two forms of detachment that Bowlby describes as pathological defenses against loss are what we recognize as the patriarchal ideals of manhood and of womanhood. Anxious attachment or compulsive caregiving is the pseudo-relationality of the selfless good woman, and detachment or compulsive self-reliance is the pseudo-independence of the heroic man. In line with Bowlby's observations, in environments hostile to expressions of vulnerability—as patriarchy is for boys—detachment tends to take the form of pseudo-independence. Whereas in insecure or engulfing relational environments, environments which are hostile to expressions of freedom—as patriarchy is for girls—detachment tends to take the form of pseudo-relationality.

Thus moves that have traditionally been considered vital to normal or normative gender development are more accurately viewed as pathological responses to loss. As well as having cultural significance in preserving the structures and politics of hierarchy and justifying or masking oppression, these gender-driven moves out of relationship may thus also serve a psychological function: protecting us against an experience of loss that has come to seem irreparable and unbearable. Moreover, it is in the name of morality—of feminine goodness and masculine honor—that these defensive responses to loss maintain the conditions of submission and dominance, silence and violence, that uphold a patriarchal order.

The initiation into the dualisms of patriarchy mirror the split between thought and emotion, self and relationship, that characterizes both detachment and anxious attachment. These splits can literally keep us from seeing the harm we suffer when concerns about manhood or womanhood impede our ability to live with integrity in relationship with others. This becomes manifest in the way we see—or more accurately are kept from seeing—the impact of patriarchy in our lives. Being unable to feel or to think about the injuries patriarchy inflicts anesthetizes us from the pain that comes with awareness, but the price of this numbness is that we are dissuaded from doing anything about its persistence.

Adam reflects, "I would have either rolled my eyes or laughed out loud if somebody had told me that the forces acting on me were forces pre-dating Aeschylus's 450 B.C.E. trilogy *The Oresteia*." His admission, made in the wake of Trump's election, hints at just how difficult it can be to recognize the injustice of the world we live in, how disruptive and disquieting it is even in the face of seemingly indisputable evidence, such as Trump's racism, misogyny, homophobia, and so on. For those of us who, like Jackie and Adam, puzzle over the disconnect between what we want to do and the way we end up acting, we contend with pressures both internal and external to avoid conflict by accepting the social narrative. By rationalizing our behavior and seeing it as in our own self-interest—telling ourselves it was better that we didn't make waves, that the rape wasn't harmful enough to justify prosecution or ruin Tom's life—or locating the loss of a friendship as just a natural part of growing up, we blind ourselves to knowledge that would demonstrate incontrovertibly that in fact patriarchy persists and is harmful.

Like some of the children in Bowlby's studies, there are people who hold on to the idea that the world is fair and caring—consistent with and responsive to their needs. To them, patriarchal codes of manhood and womanhood may appear outdated, relics rather than realities. Or they may be seen as natural, a reflection of how things are or how things should be; or taken as a manifestation of God's will. Even among people who consciously reject the patriarchal narrative, the dynamics of self-blame may be difficult to shift. They can find it easier to chalk up any failure to live according to their ideals as a sign of personal weakness that they can deal with individually rather than recognize, as Adam and Jackie came to recognize, that they were acting in response to social pressures in breaking bonds they did not want to break, or by their silence accepting the unacceptable. That is, not seeing the effects of what Adam spoke of as a framework of patriarchy and manhood, and Jackie spoke of as womanhood.

In reading my work, it has been easier for many to hear the "different voice" as a woman's voice rather than to recognize it as a human voice that comes to sound "feminine" once patriarchy sets in; easier to dismiss my work as essentialist and thereby to overlook the cultural critique that stands at its core. Easier too to focus on divisions among girls and to regard it as natural for girls to turn on one another rather than to see them, at the point when they are becoming young women, resisting a cultural framework that would divide them from one another and from themselves. That is, resisting a patriarchal order predicated on their turning against women and aligning themselves with men. Easier then to disparage rather than join the resistance.

But more insidiously, and this was our third and most surprising discovery, the gender roles of patriarchy, its codes and scripts of masculine honor and feminine goodness, ensure the move from protesting to detaching by subverting the capacity to repair relationship. They shame the human capabilities that are vital to repairing ruptures in connection, and by doing so disable our ability to stay in relationship and to reach across the boundaries of conflict and difference. More specifically, patriarchal constructions of manhood and womanhood sabotage the capacity to repair by shaming protest as unmanly and not what a good woman would do. They distort resonance so that girls' honest voices in fact come to sound shrill, rude, stupid, selfish, nasty, or crazy, too loud or too angry, and boys' vulnerable voices—the voice of love and tender compassion, of need and of care and concern— are met with contempt and derision because they sound babyish and weak or are considered passive and dependent, girly or gay.

In her paper "Understanding Patriarchy," bell hooks captures precisely the way in which patriarchal masculinity creates the rupture that cannot be repaired.[6] In order to indoctrinate boys into the rules of patriarchy, she explains, "we force them to feel pain and to deny their feelings."[7] A parallel point can be made about girls, whom we force to feel anger and then to deny their anger. She goes onto illustrate the precise workings of this mechanism in a moving and personal reflection on how patriarchal gender codes dominated her upbringing and determined how she and her brother "should be, the identities we should make."[8]

> [my brother] was taught that a boy should not express feelings. I was taught that girls could and should express feelings, or at least some of them. When I responded with rage at being denied a toy I was taught as a girl in a patriarchal household that rage was not an appropriate feminine feeling, that it should not only not be expressed but be eradicated. When my brother responded with rage at being denied a toy, he was taught as a boy in a patriarchal household that his ability to express rage was good but that he had to learn the best setting to unleash his hostility. It was not good for him to use his rage to oppose the wishes of his parents, but later, when he grew up, he was taught that rage was permitted and that allowing rage to provoke him to violence would help him protect home and nation.[9]

With this searing reflection, hooks reminds us that although race and class differences matter and intersect with gender, there are also common features to patri-archal households.

Bowlby's work shows us that the point where the psyche stops resisting the loss of connection, the point at which we sacrifice relationship for "relationships," is the moment when protest seems hopeless and loss inescapable. One only protests when there is hope of repair; without this, a healthy resistance which has taken on characteristics of a political resistance gives way to despair and then to detachment.

But the potential for protest doesn't go away. Tessie, aged eleven and a participant in one of the studies of girls' development, explains that "fighting is what makes relationships go on" because that way you learn "how the person feels" and then you know how "not to hurt their feelings."[10] Contrary to stereotypes of girls as either "nice" or "mean," pre-adolescent girls such as Tessie have a penchant to function like naturalists in the human world. Tessie describes relationships as active—contingent on a process of discovery. You have to learn how someone feels because in that way you will discover—that is come to know—how not to hurt their feelings, but the converse is also true: you have to express what you think and feel so that the other person can come to learn how not to hurt your feelings. Moreover the two are connected: the more honest you are about what you think and how you feel the more likely the other person is to be honest with you. You can also discover how to hurt their feelings, but one senses it wouldn't shock Tessie to say this. Instead, she might explain that if you want a relationship to go on, hurting someone's feelings is something you would try to avoid.

From Tessie we learn that expressing one's real thoughts and feelings, including anger, is crucial for sustaining relationships. We get a very different picture when we turn to the literature on women. A 2008 study entitled "Can an Angry Woman Get Ahead?" concluded that men who become angry are rewarded but that angry women are seen, by both men and women, as incompetent and unworthy of power in the workplace.[11] The researchers in this instance didn't consider the intersections of race and gender, or of gender with class or religion, but the truth is we know that anger in women of color tends to be judged even more harshly, seen as more volatile and unacceptable.[12] What the research does do is remind us that even in a culture where we may consciously believe in and advocate for the equality of women and a woman's right to equal treatment, we may also actively discriminate against women. And particularly women who are perceived as angry.

This is especially true in the political context. A 2010 Harvard study found that when participants saw female politicians as power-seeking and thus having agency they also saw them as having less communality (i.e. being unsupportive and uncaring), and consequently as subject to moral outrage.[13] This was not true of the participants' perceptions of or reactions to power-seeking male politicians, who were instead seen as exhibiting greater competence and agency. In a patriarchal framework, women's expression of agency and anger, their fighting for what they want or believe in—what Tessie recognizes as a way of "mak[ing] relationships go on"—is instead viewed as selfish and thus at odds with maintaining relationships. Despite all the changes in the direction of realizing greater gender equality, selflessness remains central to constructions of feminine goodness. For a woman to seek power and thus show agency still carries with it the danger that she will be perceived as a selfish woman, uncaring and thus morally compromised.

Reflecting on her campaign for the presidency, Hillary Clinton noted that "Once I moved from serving someone—a man, the president—to seeking that job on my own, I was once again vulnerable to the barrage of innuendo and negativity and attacks that come with the territory of a woman who is striving to go further."[14] It's easy to forget that before she ran for the presidency, when she served Barack Obama as his Secretary of State, Hillary Clinton was lauded as a selfless public servant and highly esteemed in the eyes of the public.[15]

The denigration of women's resisting voices, particularly in the public and political arena, has been a mainstay of patriarchal culture. In her 2017 book *Women & Power: A Manifesto*, the classicist Mary Beard traces a line from Ancient Greece to the present day, drawing parallels between the cutting out of Philomela's tongue following her rape and the telling of Senator Elizabeth Warren to sit down, to illustrate that "When it comes to silencing women, Western culture has had thousands of years of practice."[16] We add to Mary Beard's comprehensive exploration of the cultural forces that attack, demean, and silence women a psychological dimension: it is the voice of protest, the voice of angry hope that must be silenced for patriarchy to continue.

While men have been given much more leeway to speak in the public sphere, their voices—the things they are permitted to say and the way in which they are allowed to say them—have also been subjected to cultural restrictions; specifically their ability to express anything deemed feminine, most notably their vulnerability and desire for connection. In Niobe Way's studies, "no homo" was the phrase many boys came to use to hedge any depiction of emotional closeness with other boys.[17] While individual boys differed in their willingness to express desire for emotional intimacy, an overarching pattern was observed by Way. In early adolescence three-quarters of the boys in her study spoke of wanting close intimate relationships with other boys and about their confidence that these friends would not betray them by revealing their secrets or laughing at their vulnerability.[18] These boys knew the masculine stereotypes—often repeating macho mantras—and yet resisted these mantras by maintaining intimate male friendships and speaking openly about their desire for emotional closeness.[19] Trust proved crucial to resistance. In later adolescence this changed. A voice which boys had heard as natural in its open expression of love—as Justin said, speaking of his love for his best friend, "it's human nature"[20]—had come instead to be heard as "gay." Just as wanting someone to be there for you had come to sound "sissy-like." They wanted the intimacy they had when they were younger, but now knew that the emotional capacities that had proved so crucial for sustaining those connections had become a liability in relationship. In response to what had become a seemingly irresolvable crisis in connection many of these boys "'covered the sun with their hands' and claimed that their loss was inevitable or that they didn't care, didn't feel, or didn't need anybody."[21] A shift in trust in the reparability of connection underlay the shift from a healthy resistance to a psychological resistance. In this way, voices that are crucial to repairing breaks in relationships are silenced in the name of manhood and womanhood.

Thus gender creates the ruptures that cannot be repaired. The masculine taboo on tenderness, like the feminine taboo on self-expression, opens the way to a range of relational violations and betrayals. At the same time, by shaming a boy's expressions not only of hurt but also of care, by making it risky for a girl to say what she is actually feeling and thinking or to know what she does and doesn't want, these gender codes subvert our ability to recognize the ruptures in relationship, not only those we suffer but also those we inflict.

The loss of what we have called genuine or authentic relationship, such as the responsive interplay between baby and mother that we see in the YouTube video, becomes inescapable when the voices that are crucial for repairing relationship instead become a threat to relationship. What Bowlby describes as a functional anger—the anger of hope that in the face of loss fuels the effort to repair—is a protest against losing relationship, an expression of healthy resistance. But it is anger—and the challenge is to hear the hope in the protest, without dismissing the hope as unmanly in its expression of need, or in women hearing only the anger and dismissing it as hysterical or crazy, destructive and dangerous.

The rupturing of relationship that becomes irreparable when hope falls on deaf ears and protest proves ineffective then lays the ground for the shift from the "anger of hope" to the "anger of despair"—a dysfunctional anger that tends to be distorted and redirected away from the source of the loss. In a paper entitled "The Anger of Hope and the Anger of Despair: How Anger Relates to Women's Depression," Dana Jack reports a study of sixty women showing that cultural pressures on them to appear selfless operated to move anger from hope and healthy protest to despair and the "hopeless resignation central to depression."[22] By way of example, showing how often the woman's anger is turned against herself, Jack describes Jenny, a white woman age thirty-four and married with two young children. Jenny speaks of the anger that arises from trying to live up to impossible standards of selflessness. But, "Instead of viewing the anger as a signal to take action to renegotiate roles or reveal her feelings, she tries to eliminate the signal itself."[23] By redirecting the anger back on herself for her failure to be selfless, Jenny attempts to save her marriage from the feelings that she has been led to believe would destroy it.[24]

In a reverse manner, under the shadows of masculine honor, the anger of despair often becomes expressed as rage and tends to be projected outward,[25] against a more vulnerable target.[26] Moreover, this rage is used to cover vulnerability and pushes people away. In the words of Nick, one of the boys in Way's studies: "I'm not gonna get mad because you dissed me, I'm gonna get mad 'cause I missed you, but I'll probably show it to you like I'm gonna get mad because you dissed me, but it's really I'm gonna get mad because I love you and I miss you." Nick is aware that aggression and a concern with status and respect is often a cover for sadness and a concern with intimacy and betrayal.[27] Thus anger—a signal of disconnection and a spur to repairing the ruptures created by hierarchy—becomes instead a weapon, used for oppression by those on top and for self-negation by those below.

Our third discovery led us to the insight that the inability to repair relationships is connected to the inability to resist injustice. Because men and women are involved in or affected by all forms of injustice—racism, sexism, homophobia, and the like—the shaming of protest on the basis of gender undermines the human capacity to register and resist the loss of connection.

Seen in this light, gender is the lynchpin of all forms of oppression. By shaming the capacity for repair, gender closes the door to a healthy resistance to injustice. Once protest is rendered ineffective, despair and detachment become the paths we follow, harboring within ourselves the memory of what we have given up along the way.

Thus gender is not simply a matter of performance. The gender roles of patriarchy protect us from the risk of loss and rejection that comes with real intimacy and from the fear of discovering that we are unlovable. "Real men," by disconnecting from their need for love and tender care, avoid experiencing the betrayal and the pain they have come to associate with intimacy as their relationships become increasingly insensitive to expression of their emotional needs and vulnerabilities. "Good women," by detaching from their real thoughts and feelings, avoid the pain that comes from being in relationships that are unresponsive to their desires and concerns.

A Summary

The tragic irony is that defenses against loss further undermine our capacity for connection and repair. Without an honest voice, a girl or woman cannot give voice to the break in relationship or protest the loss she experiences; without a voice connected to her own desire (rather than the desires of others), she cannot give voice to her loss of pleasure; without an honest voice her silence becomes the source of rupture, rendering her in effect the still-faced mother, seemingly present but not really there—a person others cannot really connect to. But being without an honest voice, a voice connected to her own experience and desires, also protects her by avoiding a loss that may have come to feel inescapable.

Similarly, when a boy or man shields his emotional sensitivity and intelligence, he can't register the ruptures others feel, or for that matter his own feelings of loss, so in effect he both acts and suffers in silence and blindness. The internalization of patriarchal gender codes thus creates the self-perpetuating cycle of loss that Bowlby describes whereby the person who suffers the loss becomes the imposer of loss, and, we would add, the preserver of patriarchy through silence or violence.

A Summary

Naomi and Carol: Patriarchal gender roles serve a defensive function—and yet are also pathological. While it is true that the patriarchal codes of manhood and womanhood feed on a psychology of loss (the move from protest to despair to detachment), this psychology of loss in turn perpetuates the political order. Specifically in order to defend against a loss that has come to seem irreparable, we denigrate and detach from those very relational capacities necessary for repairing the ruptures that patriarchy and all forms of hierarchy create. Women who follow the path of "selfless" detachment (or anxious attachment) disavow or dissociate themselves from an honest voice—the voice that speaks from experience—thus disabling their ability to register and protest against experiences of violation or subordination. Men who follow the path of "selfish" detachment (or compulsive self-reliance) disconnect from their emotional radar, disabling their ability to empathize or care, and by doing so undermine their ability to register what is going on around them, or to repair the violations they suffer and inflict on others. A psychological pathology thus becomes a political liability because by subverting the ability to repair relationship, these dysfunctional defenses against loss not only stand in the way of love but undermine the ability to resist injustice.

PART TWO

Knowing This, Then What?

Naomi: As I read Bowlby's work I began to make sense of my own experience of loss and how it interconnected with both my adaptation to and resistance against patriarchy. Death is a rupture that cannot be repaired. No amount of protest could bring my father back. So protest gave way to despair and self-silencing, which eventually morphed into detachment. Like an emotional chameleon, I adjusted myself to the relational climate to avoid the risk of rejection or abandonment. Moreover, in a home and a culture where getting on with things was valorized as a sign of strength and goodness, any desire I did have to protest my loss was submerged.

I was told repeatedly what a good girl I was for just getting on with things—rewarded for not making a fuss and for not giving my mother any extra cause for concern. I don't recall anyone asking how I was, and if they had I probably would have said I was doing fine— so attuned was I to the sense that this was the "right" answer. I slipped relatively easily into the patriarchal mold of feminine goodness because self-silencing, caring for others rather than myself, clinging to relationships by being someone whom others wanted me to be, was something I had been doing for years.

Moreover, the patriarchal promise that good women will be rewarded with "relationships" provided they sacrifice themselves for the sake of others offered a means of avoiding the risk of abandonment, which I so desperately feared. It shored up a defense against loss I had spent my childhood crafting. Through adaptation I reduced the risk of rejection and loss, but it was also an insurance policy. If I wasn't really in relationship I could never be abandoned, the loss should it occur was happening to someone who was "not me."

By dissociating from my sense of self—my real desires, thoughts, and feelings—I began to forget the person who had been left out of the conversation. By repressing my real desires from conscious awareness they became a mystery even to myself, and so I began on one level to no longer register the impingement that came with being in "relationships" that were so unresponsive to my own needs. As a reminder, all this time in the eyes of the world I was succeeding brilliantly: I had a law degree, I had a boyfriend—an attractive Italian lawyer—I was forging a career as an international human rights lawyer and had been accepted into a Master's program at NYU school of law.

In line with Bowlby's observations, my desire for real connection, and with it my capacity to protest against false relationships, were repressed, but not lost. So the move from child to "good woman" felt on the one hand like a refuge, but on the other hand like a prison from which I longed to escape. As my sense of captivity grew, my anger mounted. And as my anger shifted to rage so my fear that self-expression would be destructive became ever more pressing. The more I became aware of my own anger at the loss of real connection, the more I felt ashamed of my real feelings—so contrary were they to my desire to be seen as good, kind and loving.

Bowlby saw anger as a healthy loss response designed to restore connection. Yet, under the shadows of a culture where women's anger is seen as a negative force—an aggressive threat to relationship—it had come to feel shameful, toxic, and dangerous. In short, the more I protested the loss of relationship the more I felt pressure to suppress my protest for the sake of having "relationships." I was trapped in a vicious cycle.

My desire for connection and protest lived on, but without the possibility for open expression it manifested in depression and anxiety—signs of psychological resistance. At twenty-five, this led me to therapy. As I described earlier, my therapist encouraged me to bring my own thoughts and feelings into relationship. He wanted me to see how my self-silencing, rooted in a fear of abandonment, was a response to the death of my father—a loss that was in fact far behind me. But I continued to silence myself in relationships—even in my relationship with my therapist. Why? Because my sense that my voice was "too loud," my opinions "too strong," my desires dangerous, was not simply "trans-ference" of a past experience onto my present reality. It was an accurate assessment of the world I lived in.

It was a response to the reality of living in a world where women are split into the good and the bad and where a woman's honest voice often sounds too loud or is dismissed as crazy, and can in fact jeopardize relationships. Seeing this led to the protest among girls entering adolescence, a protest that itself was often disguised, unless someone questioned the surface. So, for example, when Tracy, aged thirteen, a participant in one of the Harvard Project studies of girls' development—a study that had continued for five years—said: "When we were nine [meaning at the time the study began] we were stupid," it was only when Carol responded by saying that it would never have occurred to her to use the word "stupid" to describe them when they were nine because what had most impressed her about them at that time was how much they knew, that Tracy then said what she actually meant: "I mean," she said, "when we were nine, we were honest." What she thus conveyed was how between the ages of nine and thirteen, an honest voice—the voice Carol had found so striking among the girls when they were nine—had come to sound or to seem "stupid."[1]

Under the shadows of this code of feminine good behavior, I silenced my honest voice, and thus by subverting my capacity to resist and protest ruptures in relationship, I rendered loss irreparable. Thus a loss, which my therapist had shown me was far behind me, also lay clearly in the foreground. My detachment from relationship—through self-silencing and compulsive caregiving—while on the one hand pathological (because it prevented the intimacy I consciously longed for) was also psychologically protective because, by blocking the possibility of real intimacy, it shielded me from a loss that the culture rendered irreparable. If I gave up the possibility of real intimacy—by blocking my real self off—I would not feel the pain of despair once the hope for connection was inevitably dashed.

In the eyes of the world, a loss I strongly felt was not perceived as a loss since in fact I had "relationships." And if a loss cannot be seen, protest inevitably falls on deaf ears. Without resonance, my protest felt in fact stupid and so receded into silence. We had begun this project to understand why patriarchy, a system which disconnects us from the ways of relating many of us consciously long for, persists. We had found our answer. By imposing losses, shaming protest, and distorting resonance patriarchy sets us on a path from protest to despair and detachment—a psycho-logically defensive way of being and relating, which separates us from those parts of ourselves necessary for repairing the ruptures of relationship—including the injustices (the racism, sexism, and other forms of oppression) that this rupturing of relationship opens the way to.

Yet this is not the end of the story. Without resonance, my desire for real connection, my anger at living in a culture so unresponsive to my real needs and feelings, lay dormant, but was not lost. All the while a fear of loss was undermining my capacity for resistance, submerging my ability to say loudly and clearly what I really thought, a strong desire for authentic connection was pulling me in an opposing direction. It pulled me to NYU (under the pretense of furthering my career in international human rights, when somewhere in my gut

I knew this was not the real reason), and to take a class on "resisting injustice."

It was here—reading Carol's work on girls' resistance to loss and how it connected to the politics of resistance—that I found a resonance for a protest against an experience of loss that is culturally sanctioned and hidden under a framework of normalcy. And it was only by connecting my personal experience of loss—the death of my father—with this politics of injustice, that I could find my voice and also a way to do what had previously seemed inconceivable: repair the rupture with my father.

Writing about my father's death, I had an epiphany: my father was a writer, and so in writing about his loss, I was finding my way back into relationship with him. This work was my protest against loss—at once a healthy resistance to losing connection, and a political resistance against a culture that had celebrated my ability to get on with things, to not burden others with my pain, anger, or grief.

In August—in the midst of our writing this book—I returned to London for my sister's wedding. An event which marked a happy turning point in the life of our family was also tinged with an unspoken sadness. My father's absence—and thus somehow his presence—permeated the celebrations. No father to walk her down the aisle, to "give her away," or to read the "father of the bride" speech. Each absence proved a powerful reminder for all the ways my father's death marked my sister and me as different, as lacking something that society ascribes great symbolic meaning to. Something came to my awareness that I had not quite realized before. We had up until this point done our best to hide this absence from the world, not wishing our lack to be so starkly in view—not wishing to feel the pity in people's eyes, or worse, the absence of acknowledgment. I dreaded the exposure.

A few days before the wedding I was searching my mother's bedroom for a box of jewelry containing a necklace from my paternal grandmother. My mother wanted to give it to my sister as part of the "something old, something new, something borrowed, something blue" tradition. In my exploration I happened across a notebook. From my earliest childhood I can remember searching the depths of my mother's cupboards, the nooks and crannies of my father's study, for clues, trying to unravel the mystery of who my father was— who was it I had lost? Each search felt compelling and yet terrifying. What would I discover? What pain would come with knowing who he was and the magnitude of the loss? As my eyes would scan the mounds of my father's papers I could sense immediately the items of importance: the letter from an old friend, an old valentine's card to my mother, a half complete novel... these were my treasures. With hindsight, these voyages of discovery always left me feeling depleted. I never found the one thing I was unconsciously searching for: a sign from my father that he had thought of me, known me, loved me—that I had been real to him and that he had not wanted to leave me. Without this, the sense that I had not mattered—that our bond was expendable, broken irreparably—pervaded.

In my years of rummaging I had never come across this notebook. With an almost sixth sense I knew that in my hands I held something of great personal significance. The notebook was my father's diary. A diary that tracked the days from diagnosis to death—just six short months. The book was filled with a blend of the mundane and the meaningful as my father tried desperately to hold on to life (or "the little tastes of health" as he described them on the tatty sheets of this worn out pad of paper) while at the same time grappling with the tremendous fear and anger he felt toward the world and everyone in it for being healthy while he was dying. The anger and sadness spoke to me—this was my anger and sadness. How could the world have let my kind, sensitive, father be taken from me. How unjust that he should die while others lived. And how could this man suddenly so real, so full of emotion and life, be dead within just weeks of writing. In these passages my father shared with me his most vulnerable hopes, fears, and desires. As death approached his thirst for life felt palpable. This was my father's protest—against death, against leaving me. "Naomi." I read my name scribbled on one of the pages. He writes about something silly I have done—offering him up one of those "little tastes of health." My father—and the bond between us—came alive in these passages.

The timing was prescient. At precisely the moment in my life that I was protesting the loss of my father—a loss that as my therapist pointed out lay clearly behind me—I had found his own words of protest against a loss that lay clearly before him. My father's writing had not saved him from death and yet his protest had succeeded in restoring a connection that even death could not break. A brief moment of meeting. Time shifted. These words had been written over twenty-five years ago. And yet in this moment I was with my father as we both grappled with the same sadness, fears, and questions—the same strong desire to stay connected.

And so I began to see how a shared experience of loss, which by its nature separated us, was also a bond which connected us. So it turns out even death—the most permanent of losses—does not have the power to destroy relationship. My capacity to protest has the potential to maintain a connection, which until the moment of writing I believed was irreparable.

In reconnecting with the pain of loss, my sense of helplessness resurfaced—I moved from detachment back to despair. The move was a painful one, as I reconnected with all the fears and pain I had disconnected from long ago. However I was not alone—my despair found resonance in the despair of my father. And it was only by really feeling the sadness of the loss that the hope for connection resurfaced and I was able to repair our relationship. A connection was re-established based not on hierarchy—him the all-knowing father, the voice of authority, the person who, had he been alive, could have protected me or shown me the way—but on our common humanity, on the rediscovery of his voice and a voice of my own.

This move from psychological resistance to healthy resistance was a means not simply of restoring relationship with my father, but also of healing my bond with a world I had felt irreparably disconnected from. The death of my father was my scarlet letter—rendering me different and ashamed. In a therapy session I likened the sense of alienation and the need to hide it to the plague. A cross would be placed on the door of an infected family—an indication to others to keep away. My father's death was the cross on my door—rendering me different—an untouchable. The pain—were it to be expressed—would only confirm my otherness. My five-year-old self had vowed never to trust the world again. This was a vow that I would spend the next twenty-five years fighting—compelled by a strong counter desire to connect with the world, to share my real thoughts and feelings, I would repeatedly come up against an invisible wall. And then I read Carol's work.

It was as if I had found the life-line I had been searching for. The experience of loss was not the thing which separated me from the world but the thing which connected me. The voices of girls struggling against lost connection provided resonance to my personal struggle. This resonance gave me an insight into what was going on politically that I hadn't been aware of as a human rights lawyer. At the center of patriarchy was a loss that couldn't be seen or spoken of—that was hidden under the shackles of shame and cloaked in the guise of normalcy. In a culture where codes of masculine honor and feminine goodness create irreparable ruptures in relationship—where we come under immense pressure to sacrifice relationship for "relationships"—none of us is untouched by loss no matter where we sit on the social hierarchy.

This resistance against disconnection and dissociation brought me into political resistance—resistance against all the forces that had kept me quiet for so long. The forces that would render my protest self-indulgent, my desire for repair crazy and naive. The move back into a knowing based on experience and association—with myself and with others—brought me into conflict with a culture of not knowing and dissociation. In tracing the connections between the loss of my father and losses in relationship that are socially scripted and culturally prescribed, I suddenly came up against a cultural prohibition on seeing these losses of connection as losses at all.

My protest against loss was an act of resistance against a culture where differences—be they on the basis of gender, sexuality, race, or class—are said to create insurmountable barriers to connection, where the desire for domination is said to be natural and so protest is futile. My healthy resistance was an act of resistance against my mother and her embrace of the culture of "soldiering on."

The move into political resistance to the culture of patriarchy was met by pushback when we shared our work. What about race we were asked? It's a good question. Systems of oppression intersect, and patriarchy, at least in the US, is and has been for the most part white patriarchy.[2] We were asking a prior question: how can any system of oppression persist, given the relational capacities of human beings? This brought us to the realization that there has to be some mechanism for subverting these relational capacities in order for racism or any form of oppression to take hold, and patriarchy then entered as the explanation.

In saying this it is important to emphasize that we are not saying that sexism is more pernicious than racism, or that gender operates independently of race and class. What we are saying is that the gender binary and hierarchy that are foundational to patriarchy undercut human relationality and, what is perhaps most essential, subvert our ability to repair ruptures and resist injustice. How precisely this subversion occurs will differ according to race, class, sexuality, ethnicity, nationality, and the like. What cuts across these differences is the human desire to live in connection, to have a voice, to register rupture and to respond with protest.

Patriarchy is archaic we were told. Our thesis was nonsense—we were imagining losses that do not exist. Or even if they do exist this had all been said before—our protest was futile. Our protest against losses in connection, which are in fact culturally scripted, came up against a framework that preserves these losses by rendering them invisible or natural, necessary and irreparable.

In coming up against this pushback I realized just how much my detachment—silencing my honest voice—had cocooned me. Suddenly, bringing my real voice into this work felt dangerous. I felt again the dagger of pain that had hit my five-year-old self when I realized that my grief set me apart and my anger could not be spoken. Denial of a reality that was plainly before our eyes—the fact that patriarchy persists—would trigger a rage in me, which at times caused me to want to shut off and shut down. When the silence of shame tightened its grip a block would come between me and my own thoughts, I would try on words for size and none of them seemed to fit. Yet—despite some pushback—the work resonated with many. And this resonance gave me the strength to find my words and to hold on to the hope that a protest against loss would weaken the socially fabricated and psychologically upholstered walls of detachment in the face of injustice.

Bringing my personal experience of loss into a book on patriarchy was an act of political resistance in a society that draws a sharp line between the personal and the political. Trained as a lawyer, I was schooled in the need to separate reason from emotion and to hide vulnerability. I was taught that emotions—making things personal—polluted the pursuit of justice. In order to be fair we had to be blind. Our job was to apply the law impartially and objectively.

These divisions between the personal and the political, however, also disconnected me from the internal sense of justice that had propelled me into becoming a lawyer in the first place. Once I moved into a healthy resistance—resistance against the separation of my reason from my emotions—I suddenly remembered that before I had become a "good girl" I had been a "bossy girl," not afraid to say what I thought and to stand up for myself and others. I remembered that before there had been detachment there had been protest, and before there had been an overwhelming fear of loss there had been an insatiable thirst for real connection.

My feisty spirit manifested early. A perpetual sleep refuser, aged fifteen months, my mother took the bold step one night—on my father's advice—of ignoring my crying, in the hope I would get bored, tire, and fall asleep. In the morning they found me—not lying down fast asleep as they had anticipated, but standing up, clutching onto the bars of my cot, my mouth wide open, as if in mid-scream. My sister loves to tell this story, she thinks it captures something in me—a refusal to give up, a will to fight to the bitter end. It was around this time that my father began to lovingly call me "Streetfighter Suzanne" (Suzanne being my middle name).

Democracy existed in the everyday acts of rebellion: insisting my opinions be taken seriously, my needs met, my wishes considered. Injustice was not a philo-sophical or abstract issue—it was simply a matter of hating to see people with less or who were being treated unfairly (perhaps because I knew first-hand how desperately unfair and painful it felt not to have what others did). Speaking truth to power (and what is the cry "it's not fair" so often heard from the mouths of children if not that?) was simply doing what felt right and good, protecting the interests of those I cared about—including my own. I had experienced the death of my father as a great injustice, an experience which bestowed on me a sharp sensitivity to the pain and suffering of others, a sensitivity that would compel me to act. Aged six, my mother found me one day taking clothes out of the cupboard to lend to children in my class who, not having gym kits, were forced to do gym class in their underwear. The unfairness of this rule hit me on a visceral level—I could not bear to see some children treated differently from others, shamed because they had less. As a child I had refused to accept unfairness as just the way things are.

Looking back I am saddened to think about the friendships I betrayed along the road to becoming a good woman. At precisely the same time I disavowed my own voice I distanced myself from those girls who refused to do the same—seeing their expressions of anger as threatening, of self-assertion as selfish and of desire as shameful. In my striving to be seen as a good woman I had not only betrayed myself, I had distanced myself from the other fearless, bossy, angry determined girls who had been my allies.

In the end, I discovered that in order to realize my desire for justice, the desire that had driven me to law in the first place, I needed to combine my understanding of the political with an understanding of the psychological forces that sustain injustice. So I embarked on psychoanalytic training.

Carol: Retracing my steps, I come to a critical juncture in my life and work. Implicit in my first book, *In a Different Voice*, were the questions: how had a voice that was recognizably human come to sound "different"? Different from what? And how had a voice that joins reason with emotion and the self with relationship, that is embodied rather than disembodied, come to sound "feminine"?

After writing *In a Different Voice*, I embarked on what at the time struck me as a straightforward inquiry. I would fill in a missing stretch of psychological history by connecting women with girls. Joseph Adelson, editor of the 1980 *Handbook of Adolescent Psychology*, had noted the omission: "Adolescent girls have simply not been much studied ... To read the psychodynamic literature on adolescence has, until very recently, meant reading about the psychodynamics of the male youngster writ large."[3]

What had been missed by not studying girls? Adelson cautioned that the psychology of adolescence contained a subtle but pervasive "masculine bias," manifest in the overemphasis on separation and achievement and a corresponding neglect of nurturance, intimacy, and love.[4] The psychology of adolescence was not simply the psychology of the male youngster writ large. It was a psychology steeped in a culture that was deeply gendered, where separation and achievement were seen as masculine and relationships and love were considered feminine, a culture where the masculine was elevated and the feminine at once idealized and devalued. To paraphrase Adelson, the psychology of adolescence was the psychology of patriarchy writ large.

In the fall of 1981, with a group of graduate students, I began what became the Harvard Project on Women's Psychology and Girls' Development—a series of studies that continued for over ten years. The project involved hundreds of girls between the ages of seven and eighteen, zeroing in on their experiences in coming of age and exploring relationships between women and girls at this time. The research took place in a range of school and after-school settings, private and public, urban and suburban, with girls from a variety of ethnic and social class backgrounds. With my students I co-authored and co-edited five books on our findings, including *Meeting at the Crossroads*, a *New York Times* notable book of the year in 1992, which focused on women meeting girls and girls meeting women at the crossroads of girls' adolescence, and *Between Voice and Silence*, which highlighted the experiences of working-class girls at risk for school dropout and early pregnancy. In this book we also described the Women and Race retreats held in conjunction with the research in an effort to heal rather than perpetuate divisions among women, in particular women working with girls. Girls are half the population in every generation, as one of the retreat participants observed.

It was listening to girls narrate their experiences in coming of age that led me to write about resistance. At first I was taken aback by coming upon something at once so familiar to me and yet surprising. And then I realized—what had been missed by not studying girls was this resistance. Seeing girls' resistance, I saw the culture they were resisting. In coming of age, girls were resisting the culture of patriarchy, that would force them to choose between having a voice or having relationships.

This is the framework implicit in *In a Different Voice*—the framework in which a quintessentially human voice sounds "different." Different from a voice that had come to sound natural or objective. Different because it joins self with relationships, thoughts with emotions, the mind with the body, and "feminine" because in the gender codes of patriarchy, relationships and emotions are women's preoccupations.

Girls had shown me the answers to my three questions. It is in patriarchy that a human voice becomes a different voice, a feminine voice and also a resisting voice. This was the signal contribution of the studies with girls.

I will always remember the woman who first alerted me to the shift in the framework. It was early on in my research but even now I see her leaning toward me and hear the slight edge of conspiracy as she asks: "Do you want to know what I think, or do you want to know what I really think?"[5] I had asked her to respond to a moral dilemma and her response told me something it would take me years to fully comprehend: she had learned to think about morality in a way that differed from how she really thought. She had been initiated into a way of thinking that was not how she actually thought, and she was aware of the difference. Which voice did I want to hear? The voice that said how she thought about morality, or a different voice—the voice that said what she really thought?

My response was telling. I knew instantly what she was talking about.

In the mid-1980s when I was up for tenure at Harvard, a thoughtful member of my department took me aside. She told me that the committee reviewing my work wanted to talk with me about methods. They thought I didn't understand the statistical concept of regression around the mean. When I started to explain that in fact I did understand regression around the mean but that my research had not been statistical, she stopped me. "Let them help you," she advised.

Reflecting on this conversation with my dean, who was also a friend, I was incredulous. "*They*"—my colleagues in human development and psychology— "want to talk with *me* about methods? They who had left out half the sample?" The dean was clearly on my side. "Don't go there," she said gently. She was advising me to be strategic, to be careful about when and how I spoke, in part because she wanted my voice to be heard.

"Don't say that ... People won't appreciate it if you say that ... Shhhhh ... ." In the days when I was spending time with girls, I would repeatedly hear them advised by women not to speak. Not to say what they were actually feeling and thinking but to listen for what others want to hear. Crossing from girlhood into becoming young women, they were being initiated by women who were speaking from their own experience, who knew first-hand the costs of speaking and not speaking. But in the course of this initiation, girls were moving from what for many had been a sure-footed terrain (however rocky) into a realm of uncertainty. In the transcripts of our interviews with girls, this move was flagged by the phrase "I don't know." Girls were entering a framework in which there are many incentives not to say what they see, not to listen to what they hear or know what they know. A framework that hinges on women being selfless—responsive to others but seemingly without a voice or desires of our own. A framework in which a woman who speaks for herself is "selfish" or reckless.

In a Different Voice had created such resonance. It took everyone including me by surprise. But the research with girls proved far more radical, because it exposed the roots of the problem: there is a tension between human development and the culture of patriarchy.

Your work is poetry not research, I was told by the woman who was my department chair at Harvard. I took it as a compliment, overlooking the slur. My research was feminism not psychology, politics not science, my graduate students were told by members of the Committee on Degrees that had rejected their thesis proposals. By then it was the mid-1990s. I had been tenured for ten years but my work was still being placed within the very framework it had exposed and called into question—the framework within which the "different voice" was heard not as a human voice but as a woman's voice because it was emotional (as well

109

as thoughtful), and embodied and responsive, relational rather than detached.

In the spring and summer of 2000, in the run up to the Gore vs. Bush election, the gender gap in voting loomed large. It had been increasing steadily since 1980, reflecting perhaps the emphasis on voice in second-wave feminism that had encouraged women not only to claim their rights but also to listen to themselves. In 1996, for the first time since suffrage, women's votes had elected the president.

In May of 2000, in a cover story for the *Atlantic*, Christina Hoff Sommers, a philosopher who had become a resident scholar at the conservative American Enterprise Institute, accused me of waging a "war against boys," the title of her forthcoming book.[6] More insidiously, she had enlisted a Harvard undergraduate who, on the pretext of writing a paper for one of his classes, had called my office and asked my assistant for access to my interview transcripts. I was not privy to their conversation. In fact, the transcripts were available at the Murray Research Center at Radcliffe, accessible to qualified researchers though not necessarily to random undergraduates. But whatever transpired, I was taken aback when I read in the *Atlantic* that I had no data, that my claims were unsubstantiated, that my work was politics not science. The rising gender gap in US elections was, in the eyes of Christina Hoff Sommers, an indication of the extent to which women had been misled by feminists.

A woman wrote to me at Harvard, returning her paperback copy of *In a Different Voice* and asking that I refund the $5.95 she had spent in purchasing my book.

I could see the politics at work. With the election coming up, if women could be dissuaded from listening to a different voice (a voice that was not patriarchal), if women could be led to believe that feminists were engaged in a war against boys, then presumably the gender gap in voting would disappear. Women's votes would no longer differ from men's and, given the proclivity of men to vote Republican, Bush would be elected president. The timing of Sommers' article was brilliant. If she could dislodge women's confidence in themselves and instill in women the fear that in speaking for themselves and advocating for girls they are hurting boys, she might shift the vote just enough to undo the effects of the women's movement and restore a patriarchal order.

The year 2000 was a watershed in US politics. Given our pride as Americans in our democratic institutions and values, the disputed election and the politically polarized Supreme Court vote that decided the presidency were thorns in our side. How could we continue to uphold our view of ourselves as a democracy and also know what we knew? The predicament was ripe for detachment and dissociation.

I had been baffled by how, despite the resonances so many people found in my work, the framework it challenged remained sturdily in place. At the very beginning of *In A Different Voice*, on page 2 of the introduction, I say: "The different voice I describe is characterized not by gender but theme."[7] In the opening pages of *Meeting at the Crossroads*, Lyn Mikel Brown and I write: "It is important to emphasize that about 20% of the girls (in our study) come from working-class

111

families and are attending the school on scholarship and that about 14% of the girls are of color."[8]

It made no difference. The framework was too powerful. It was easier to speak of women's voices as different from men's than to hear women's voices shifting the framework. It was easier to focus on divisions among women and to see how white girls could be blinded by their privilege than to hear girls resisting a culture that would divide them from one another and from themselves.

I had reached a turning point. I could continue doing what I had been doing. The project with girls and women, the study with young boys and their fathers, and the work with couples in crisis had all raised questions that prompted further exploration. But I was gripped more by the tension between the resonance people found in the work and the tenacity of the framework it challenged.

In the fall of 1998, I had gone to New York to spend the year as the Visiting Meyer Research Professor at NYU School of Law. At Harvard, I had been teaching in the department of human development and psychology. Within psychology, resistance has negative connotations: resisting going to therapy, resisting going to school, resisting separations that are a necessary part of growing up, not facing the truth, not facing reality. As in resisting knowing that your father is dead, or that in fact you are angry.

Coming to NYU, coming back to New York where I had grown up, I was aware of a shift. I was coming to see—not at a glance but straight on—the framework that my work was coming up against. Teaching at the law school made it easier because there the existence of a normative ethical framework was not in question. That first year at NYU, I taught with Peggy Cooper Davis, whose book *Neglected Stories*[9] focused on the 14th Amendment and how following Reconstruction the constitution had finally offered protection to marital and family ties that had been severed under slavery. I also taught with David Richards, whose book, *Women, Gays, and the Constitution*[10] introduced me to Abolitionist Feminism. In this setting, it became easier to see how a framework could change and to explore the political ramifications of what from a psychological standpoint was a healthy resistance to losing relationship.

With *In a Different Voice* I had broken a silence. Finding resonance in the voices of the women who participated in my research, finding resonance also in the voices of artists (the book opens with a scene from Chekhov), I had found a way to say what I really thought about morality and human development. I had moved from a stance of detachment to one of engagement, from dissociation to a healthy resistance.

By 2002, with *The Birth of Pleasure*, my resistance had become indelibly political. By then, it had become clear to me that the voice the "different voice" differed from was a patriarchal voice, a voice that spoke from a privileged male standpoint and was heard not as a voice but as a statement of fact: the voice of truth and moral authority. In the opening pages of *The Birth of Pleasure*, I use the word patriarchy for the first time in my work, contrasting it not with matriarchy but with democracy[11] and quoting the poet Jorie Graham: "How

113

far is true / enough? / How far into the / earth / can vision go and / still be / love?"[12]—because my research on development, which began as a quest for truth, had turned into an inquiry about love.

The project with girls and women, and the study with young boys and their fathers that followed, had illuminated in startling detail just how it is and also when and why we can come to think in a way that differs from how we really think and feel. I saw how, when the framework shifts, dissociation can set in and we can come literally not to see what is right in front of our eyes or know what deep inside ourselves we know. I found myself drawing a new map—a radical geography of love, where love is contingent on seeing and knowing rather than on blindness and silence.

Two observations stay with me from this time. Both took me by surprise. The first was my discovery that by questioning a framework that seemed securely in place, I would hear a voice I had not imagined. Beneath a culturally scripted patriarchal voice, a human voice— relationally cadenced and emotionally intelligent—had been held in silence, as though waiting to be called forth. The research with girls had alerted me to listen for the conversation under the conversation. "Is that true? ... Do you really believe that? ... Do you really feel that way?," I found myself asking adolescent girls when in response to a question they said something that struck me as rehearsed or canned or banal or pathetic, as when Sheila said, "I don't like myself enough to look out for myself." Then I would hear the word "Actually ...," as the preface to a girl telling me what she really thought and felt, or, in Sheila's case, how in fact she looked out for herself.

114

But it wasn't just girls. When Phil, a man whose marriage was in crisis, said that for him "the ultimate nightmare" was "her in the arms of another man," I asked him: "Why is this the ultimate nightmare?"[13] My question called forth a voice I hadn't anticipated: beneath the patriarchally scripted voice, there was a different voice. Again the word "really" signaled the shift: "The ultimate nightmare really for me was to never have the opportunity to show her how I really feel and to be a family man, to open my heart and to love her."[14] It struck me that Phil knew what was really going on in his marriage.

Reflecting on my questioning of the patriarchal script in which girls suffer from low self-esteem and a man's worst nightmare is his wife's infidelity, I see how my very asking of the question provided a resonance which turned out to be crucial in freeing a voice that otherwise would remain unheard and whose very existence would be disputed. I realized at once how easy it is to expose the framework and also how easy it would be to miss the voices that this framework renders shameful and drives into silence. I also realized how often what passes in research for objectivity (or neutrality on the part of the researcher) serves to maintain the status quo. By leaving the prevailing cultural framework unchallenged or unquestioned, research in the name of objectivity holds that framework in place.

The second observation also surprised me. In the ten years I spent studying girls' development, I worked very closely with women. The work we did together was transformative. The Women Teaching Girls/Girls Teaching Women retreats initiated by teachers and administrators at the Laurel School in Cleveland, and subsequently held with middle school teachers and principals in the Boston public schools, created communities that invigorated women and encouraged them to move from detachment to engagement, from dissociation to healthy resistance. The Harvard Project produced five books documenting what we had learned about human development and the human condition by listening to girls and women. The Women and Race retreats took on the thorny question of divisions among white, black, and brown-skinned women—most pointedly the question: where were you when they came for me in the middle of the night? The voices of brown, black, and white girls became the spur to shifting our focus from past to future: from recrimination to transformation, from detachment and dissociation to protest and repair.

The observation that stays with me is that in all three instances—the Teaching retreats, the Harvard Project research group, and the Women and Race retreats—at the point where the potential for transformation had become palpable, when change was not only in the air but had begun to take hold on an institutional level, the groups ended abruptly. It was not just that conflict had broken out among the women. We had dealt with conflict before. It was that this time we couldn't talk about what had happened. In each of the three cases the split followed what was taken as a betrayal, an action that called into question whether women can count on other women to stay with them when the going gets rough and trust the authority of their own experience.[15]

116

Knowing This, Then What?

I felt an urgency about taking the next step. I knew how to call forth a healthy resistance but not how to sustain that resistance once it became political and came up against the forces, both internal and external, that would drive it into silence. I knew that I could start a process of transformation most anyplace by building what my colleague Normi Noel, who works in theater, calls a "cello world"—a resonant space where the voice is resounded in a way that encourages a person to say out loud what they know deep down to be true. "I don't want her ever to lose that," a father said of his lively and outspoken eleven-year-old daughter, cherishing his relationship with her. "Then you're involved in social change," I told him. Because by then it was clear to me that the pre-adolescent girls, and the four- and five-year-old boys whose voices had such human resonance, were up against something real: the crude, powerful, and mysterious force that Tolstoy had described, a patriarchal framework that, as Adam reflected, is older than *The Oresteia*, that acts on us and that we enact "without a conscious thought."

It was the connection to Bowlby following Naomi's question about loss that in the end illuminated a mechanism of such precision that it took my breath away. In my mind, I hold the image of an exquisite fourteenth-century table fountain that I saw in the Cleveland Museum of Art. I had marveled at the intricacy of its design. Water coming from small jets at the top of the fountain would cause the water wheels below to turn, which then would ring the tiny bells. Given the human desire to live in relationship, given the relational capacities that are integral to our humanity,

117

it is necessary that these capacities be impeded or stunted in order to establish and maintain hierarchy. As the YouTube video of the baby and still-faced mother shows, in the normal course of things we instantly register the loss of connection and move to repair the rupture. The brilliance of patriarchy and the psychological function, if I can put it that way, of its gender codes become transparent once we recognize that by forcing a break in relationship and then shaming the moves to repair the rupture, these gender codes make the loss of relationship irreparable.

As Bowlby observed, in environments where there is no possibility for responsive relationship, detachment becomes adaptive. And so, in different ways, we adapt to the culture of patriarchy by detaching ourselves from relationship, whether by becoming seemingly self-sufficient, independent, and not needing others, or by becoming seemingly selfless, without a voice or needs and desires and perceptions of our own. We may tell ourselves that what we are doing is honorable and good, but somewhere within ourselves is that baby in the YouTube video who knows this isn't true.

When I think back now to what in retrospect I recognize as a time of upheaval, the time I moved from Cambridge to New York, it is clear to me that I had come to see something it would take me years to comprehend. Over and over again I had been surprised to discover how little it takes to free a voice from captivity. It challenged everything I had been taught about human psychology and research methods. And then I was stunned by the forces marshaled to hold in place a framework that keeps us from seeing the obvious and from saying what we know deep inside to be true about life.

Finding Resonance, Repairing Ruptures

Naomi and Carol: The price of keeping loss safely behind us is a sacrifice of love and of democracy, which like love depends on equal voice and responsive engagement. However, within the psychology of loss that holds patriarchy in place are the seeds of resistance and transformation. Our natural response to loss is protest. Providing resonance for this protesting voice, hearing the voice of angry hope as the voice of healthy resistance—a human voice, neither unfeminine in its anger nor unmanly in its expression of vulnerability and care—is a key to repairing the ruptures in relationship on which patriarchy and all forms of injustice rely.

In highlighting the importance of resonance we refer to the way in which the sounding board of an instrument enlarges and enhances its sound, and how what we say is affected by what comes back to us. How we are responded to when we speak, whether what we say resonates with others or falls on deaf ears, affects what we can and will say. In the absence of resonance, or when what comes back is so distorting that we can't recognize ourselves in people's responses to us, we not only experience an absence of connection with others but also perhaps a loss of trust in our ability to communicate what we want to say.

However, as the studies of development have shown, the voice that protests the loss of relationship is a voice that resists patriarchy, and although it may be repressed or driven into silence, it is not lost. The examples drawn from the research attest that although the resisting voice may be silent, it can be called forth by what on the face of it is a simple question: "Why is this the ultimate nightmare?" or "Do you really feel that way?" Questions that disrupt the surface by creating an opening in the patriarchal narrative.

The very asking of these questions was a protest against disconnection which shifted the resonance. In the case of Phil, the man whose marriage was in crisis, and Sheila, who initially hid the fact that in fact she did look out for herself, this shift in resonance then made it possible for them to say what otherwise had felt forbidden or shameful. Or perhaps what they had assumed could not be heard or understood. In fact, Sheila knew the price that she paid in looking out for herself by not speaking truthfully; she had sacrificed her desire for honesty in relationships. Just as Phil knew the price he had paid in his marriage by never being able to tell his wife how he really felt—by not opening his heart and loving her.

Thus we came to see how the politics of patriarchy subverts the psychology of protest and resistance to loss, while at the same time this psychology keeps on creating an opening, an opportunity for political transformation. Put simply, our relational desires and capacities, which are present in rudimentary form from the very outset, keep opening a potential for love and democracy while the politics of patriarchy keep shutting it down. Knowing this, the solutions become twofold: one, joining the healthy resistance and by doing so encouraging the psychology that would transform the political; and two, naming and taking on the cultural and political forces that, by subverting the capacity to repair, drive a healthy resistance into despair and detachment, thus paving the way to oppression and injustice.

Leaving Patriarchy

Carol: The road went down. On either side, the sculpted sands of the desert, like a scene from *Lawrence of Arabia*. Except, this time, it was women crossing into what was in many ways, and yet also not, unfamiliar territory. Not the territory of our families, our cultures, our religions, our social classes or skin colors, our alignments with fathers. Rather we had come together to reconcile with one another as the daughters—the children actually, because men had joined us—to reconcile as the children of Sarah and Hagar, the Biblical foremothers in the Abrahamic traditions.

Israelis and Palestinians, Arabs and Jews, Jews and Muslims, young and old women, religious and secular women, women from moderate settlements in the West Bank, women from the hip urban enclaves of Tel Aviv. It was the fall of 2017. We were crossing the desert, making our way to the tent of reconciliation. We were women leaving patriarchy, along with the men who had come with us on this Journey to Peace.

The day was hot. I had been told to prepare for the scorching desert and was wearing white, the color worn by members of Women Wage Peace—a movement that began in 2014, in response to the war in Gaza. This cannot go on, a group of women said, gathering in Tel Aviv; this conflict must stop. We need a new language. An agreement must be negotiated, and following UN Security Council resolution 1325, women must be involved at each step of the process.[1]

Donna Kirshbaum, a cellist, a rabbi, and one of the women who organized the march, had brought me the turquoise scarf worn by the women in the movement, along with a turquoise baseball cap. I watched her drape her scarf over her cap to form a make-shift shelter as we headed out of the welcoming tent and into the desert.

Fear no more the heat of the sun—the line from *Cymbeline* that runs through *Mrs Dalloway*. It was indeed hot, but the fear instilled in me by American friends who had cautioned me to be careful, to not take risks, and also by one of my Israeli companions who was anxious on the drive down from Jerusalem, had dissipated. Whatever brakes had kept us from acting in concert with one another as women had been released, and with that release came a feeling of exuberance.

We were in Area C, a part of Israel where Palestinians can come without a permit. We were at the lowest point on earth, the Dead Sea off to one side and ahead in the distance, the hills of Jordan. Thousands of women—the estimates varied: three to five thousand Palestinians, five to seven thousand Israelis. Either way it was impressive and made a statement. Women were joining as women across all the lines of division to wage peace, to press their political leaders, Abbas and Netanyahu, to negotiate an agreement between Israel and the Palestinian Authority, to make ending the conflict their highest priority.

Leaving Patriarchy

In addition to the heat, I felt the presence of the women around me. Israelis mostly in white, some with their heads covered, and Palestinians, most with head scarves, some wearing abayas, all looking joyous. Because we had come together, as the Beatles would have it, with a common intention; however disparate our lives, however different our backgrounds and our commitments, we had in common the determination that the time had come for women to wage peace.

It was the decision to take things into their own hands that mobilized the women of Israel and Palestine to come together as women across vast divides. "Why women and why now?" Donna Kirshbaum had asked in the piece she wrote in 2014, shortly after the Gaza war. Because there was "an urgent need for different language." A need to ask a different question: not what is just but how to respond.[2]

Because it was no longer possible for women to sit by and watch efforts at negotiation fail without attempting to do something *as women* to stop the conflict and bring an end to the destruction. Because it was impossible not to take action *as women* to stop the sacrifice of children. Because *as women* we had for the most part been relegated to the sidelines; because *as women*, given our different experiences and situation, we might bring a different voice into the conversation.

There was, from the beginning, a commitment that there be a diversity of women, and looking around, that's what I saw. We were women waging peace and this journey had led us to a place of reconciliation, a tent in the desert large enough to accommodate the thousands of women who had come to reconcile with one another in the conviction that however painful the past, it was possible to do things differently. We had come together as women to protect the future, to protect the lives of our collective children.

We marched the few kilometers from the welcoming tent to the tent of reconciliation, the road leading further down. I had followed Donna in using the cap as a frame for the scarf, but still the heat was scorching. Sweat ran down my face. I noticed a woman wearing high heels under her abaya and applauded her daring. And then, nestled in the sand below and off to one side, its top rising over the dunes, the tent of reconciliation appeared. Two tents actually, large enough when joined to accommodate the thousands of women, Israelis and Palestinians, Jews and Arabs, who had committed themselves to end the conflict.

A tall order, my American friends had said.

It was early October, a Sunday—the first day of the week in Israel. The Journey to Peace had been making its way through Israel starting in the west near the Gaza border, moving from the south to the north and then to the east, to the Judean desert. That night, Sunday night, the journey would end with a rally in Jerusalem. As it turned out, 30,000 people gathered in the park not far from the prime minister's residence—the equivalent to 1.14 million in the US in terms of percentage of the population. There was a stage and a program of speakers and singers. Yael Deckelbaum and her band played the "Prayer of the Mothers," the song she had composed for the 2016 March of Hope, also organized by Women Wage Peace. Everything was said both in Arabic and in Hebrew, sometimes also in English. Among the speakers, Liora Hadar, a religious woman from a settlement in Samaria, the northern West Bank, said: "I believe change can come if thousands of women decide together they simply won't live under the conflict anymore." Shachiv Shnaan, a Druze former member of the Knesset who had lost his son Kamil, a policeman, in a terrorist attack, said: "We've suffered much. Israeli and Palestinian families have lost their loved ones and we're left with wounds that cannot heal. I'm here to say: We choose life. We're allowed to say it loud: we are lovers of peace." And Huda Abu Arqoub, Regional Director of the Alliance for Middle East Peace, said: "As a Hebron resident and someone in contact with the people of Gaza, I'm here to tell you Gaza residents also believe in an end to the hostilities and are crying out for peace ... Wars don't have any winners. We're neither Palestinian nor Israeli—but mothers who'll do everything for a better future for our children."

We are women ... we are families who have lost their loved ones ... we choose life ... we are lovers of peace ... we are mothers who'll do everything for a better future for our children.

A tall order, yes. It wasn't that I didn't agree. But as my friends would explain how hopeless the situation was and how naive it was to think that women could accomplish this and in this way (refusing to advocate for a specific solution to the conflict, beyond the determination that an agreement to end it must be reached and that a diversity of women must be involved at every stage of the process), all I could say was: Well, everything else has failed so why not try this. To which they actually agreed. Why not?

There was no reason.

In the tent in the desert, pipes strung along the canvas ceiling dripped a cooling mist. There was water and food and music. I was the only American among the four women who had been asked to speak; the others were a Palestinian peace activist, an Israeli Jewish novelist, and an Israeli Arab educator. We spoke different languages but our voices blended into a tapestry of reconciliation. The women sitting in front of the low platform on which the four of us were seated responded to all that was spoken, including the pain suffered by Sarah and by Hagar: the pain they had caused one another, Sarah by being the one who was chosen, Hagar by being the one who could bear children. Why is it always a zero-sum game?, I found myself wondering, thinking how often in the Bible there is one who is chosen and one who is not, thinking of my friend Tova Hartman who just a few nights before had been speaking about Esau, whose birthright had been stolen by his brother Jacob, his mother's favorite, and Esau's question to Isaac, his father: "Do you have only one blessing?"

For all too long too many of us had succumbed to the myth that there is only one blessing—never enough to go around. If we were now to reconcile as the daughters of Sarah and Hagar, our Jewish and Muslim foremothers, we had to acknowledge not only the pain they had suffered but also the pain they had caused. Because although women have for the most part not waged war, we were not simply bystanders. We were the mothers, and however indirect our relation to power, we did have a hand in what happened. Or in any case, we did not stand in the way or lie down in the street to stop it.

126

"I hope you don't write this," a woman said after I spoke. She was Israeli, Jewish, which perhaps made her feel free to say what she had come up to say. Because I too am Jewish, and, as she told me, she was a great fan of my work and assigned my books in her classes. "I hope you won't write what you said about Sarah," she repeated, concerned that then people would blame her.

What I had said was that Sarah had started something which then snowballed: the willingness to sacrifice children for some higher purpose or cause. It was Sarah who urged Abraham, her husband, to send Hagar and Ishmael into the desert where presumably they would die, since until God miraculously appeared and produced a well in the sand, there was no water. My friend Tova, in the same conversation in which we had spoken of Esau, said that in the Bible Sarah disappears once the *akedah*, the binding—or sacrifice—of Isaac, begins. Once Abraham sets out to sacrifice Isaac, Sarah disappears from the story—we hear nothing of her until she is dead, when Abraham buries her in Hebron. But in the Midrashim, the Biblical commentaries, when Sarah learns that her husband is preparing to sacrifice their son, she screams.

In the *dvar torah*, the reflection on the weekly Torah portion that Tova gave in her shul on Rosh Hashanah, the Jewish new year, she said that in that moment Sarah dies because there is no more oxygen, no air. Because that is the moment when Sarah realizes that what she had done in her willingness to sacrifice Ishmael, Hagar's son, so that her son Isaac would be the favored son, the chosen son, had in fact snowballed. The sacrifice of children was continuing, and now it was her son who

127

would be sacrificed, also in the service of a putatively higher end, to prove Abraham's devotion to God—although once again, in the Bible story, God intervenes to stop the sacrifice of children.

In waging peace and opposing war, women were coming together as women to say "Enough!" This has to stop. We will no longer collude in the sacrifice of children in the name of whatever higher purpose or cause.

As women waging peace, we had come together as women to help men by opposing war.

Long after the march, I continue to open my computer or search on my phone for the photograph of the unbroken line of women making our way through the desert toward the tent of reconciliation. It is a photograph of women leaving patriarchy.[3]

Why women and why now? Donna Kirshbaum took up these questions in 2014, the year Women Wage Peace began. By 2017, it was the largest grassroots peace movement in Israel. Under the tent on the shores of the Dead Sea, Huda Abu Arqoub, the Palestinian from Hebron, said it was time—time "for women to make their mark because women matter, because women are inclusive, because women gave so much trust to the leaders here and the leaders failed us."[4] Patriarchy had failed women. But within patriarchy, women also have an advantage. Because typically girls are initiated later than boys, we are more likely to recognize patriarchy for what it is: a voice or a framework, a way of seeing and speaking about things rather than how things are.

This is what Donna referred to in addressing the questions why women and why now: Because initiation into patriarchy with its gender codes and hierarchy requires "losing one's authentic [read human] voice and dissociating from what we know deep down to be true about life—that it is interdependent and always has an emotional component." And because "girls tend to resist this initiation longer than boys, often by ten years or so."[5] I am quoting Donna, who is citing my research.

"A Call to Peace" was hand-delivered to members of the Knesset on the opening day of the parliament's 2017 winter session. Members of Women Wage Peace had formed themselves into a kind of women's knesset to bring a different and more hope-filled voice into the typically despair-filled discussions of the conflict, buoyed by the conviction that there is a different way. Along the route of the Journey to Peace, the marchers had been joined by local politicians and nationally elected officials. Mayors had spoken at the rallies held in their cities, including the mayors of right-wing cities such as Dimona and Tiberias as well as the mayor of Tel Aviv. Now every Monday, diverse women from Women Wage Peace would join the politicians by coming to the Knesset and asserting the priority of negotiating an agreement to end the conflict.

Why women? Because as women, there are things that we know that can be helpful. As girls we have a longer period of grace before we are initiated into the gender codes of womanhood and thus, as Kirshbaum— an American now living in the Middle East—put it, we "generally have more time to establish both a richer vocabulary and a better developed foundation for an authentic voice before it is lost to the demands of patri-archy." Because "We are women who believe that our voices deserve to be heard and that a richly democratic culture could and should flourish here"; because, as women, we "learn to listen for the conversation *under* the conversation," that is, we "learn to identify a speaker's authentic voice often buried under the highly-scripted one learned in a patriarchal culture that expects both men and women to lose 'their basic capacity to relate'."[6] Because it is usually not until a later age that we begin to dissociate from what we know deep down to be true about life. Because as women we have not been taught as men have been taught that violence is the royal road to honor, survival, and power. Because as women we know this is not true.

Naomi: Because as women we are so trained to listen, we are more likely to hear the human voice as different from the patriarchal voice—but we're not supposed to know this.

Reading Carol's description of the Journey to Peace, I am moved to wonder whether the path these women are charting in fact provides a road map out of patriarchy. War is the starkest and most violent manifestation of the cycle of loss that underpins patriarchy: violent conflict shatters relationships (at both a societal and familial level), and in turn this threat of destruction is used to justify further violence, often in the name of restoring masculine honor and protecting women and children. Women Wage Peace envisions a way out—a path to reconciliation that leads not simply through debate or persuasion, but through dialogue and listening; not through the doling out of punishments or blame, but by communalizing shared experience of suffering and loss.

In waging peace, they are protesting the losses inherent in war. The very conflict that is said to divide these women thus becomes the bond that unites them.

Lest we underestimate the magnitude of what Women Wage Peace aspires to, it is worth taking a moment to reflect on the very real obstacles that stand in the way. The members of Women Wage Peace have each, to varying degrees and in different ways, had their lives ravaged by the conflict. These are women and men who have lost children, siblings, friends, and lovers to war. It is not difficult to imagine the level of rage, despair, and distrust that such loss and injustice leave in their wake. In this treacherous terrain, the path to peace and reconciliation is fraught with pain and seemingly insurmountable obstacles. We may find ourselves wondering, how is it possible to find empathy for the person or people you deem responsible for your suffering? We may even question whether empathy is the appropriate response, wondering whether resisting injustice requires something more forceful in the way of calling people to account.

Women Wage Peace teaches us the necessity for what we and our colleagues have come to call radical listening,[7] a form of listening that goes to the root of what is being said and holds a potential for transformation. It is a form of listening driven by curiosity, where the goal is to understand, not to condone or to excuse. And understanding is not a zero-sum game—we can understand another's experience without letting go of our own or losing sight of the pain or anger their actions may have caused us. In this way, listening becomes a radical act. It can move us away from rigidly held positions when we open ourselves and take

131

into ourselves the experiences and suffering of others. In listening, we open ourselves to discovery—to the unknown, and also potentially to the recognition of a common humanity. By forging a path toward reconciliation through a shared desire to end the cycle of loss, Women Wage Peace has found a way to move from the anger of despair to the anger of hope.

In October 2017, the week that Carol and the women waging peace were marching through the desert, finding connection in the common experience of pain and loss wrought by war, women across the globe were coming together to protest a more hidden assault—the abuse of women and the violation of their bodies. On October 5, the *New York Times* released an article detailing decades of sexual assaults on women by Harvey Weinstein.[8] The following Sunday, the actress Alyssa Milano took to Twitter to urge any woman who had been sexually harassed or assaulted to add two words to her Twitter feed: "Me too."

The MeToo campaign had been created by Tarana Burke in 2007, as a grassroots movement to reach sexual assault survivors in underprivileged communities. Burke told *Ebony*, "it was a catchphrase to be used from survivor to survivor to let folks know that they were not alone and that a movement for radical healing was happening and possible."[9] Milano tweeted, "If all the women who have been sexually harassed or assaulted wrote 'Me too' as a status, we might give people a sense of the magnitude of the problem."[10] Her call to arms moved millions of women—and some men—to break their silence, telling their stories of abuse and harassment.[11] With this communalization of suffering, there was new resonance for a voice of angry hope—a voice that had been forced into silence by a culture that has valorized powerful men and shamed their victims. The more women who spoke out about their experiences of sexual harassment the more others found the courage to speak up and say what they knew. Some men joined their protest—some by revealing their own experience of sexual harassment and abuse at the hands of more powerful men, others by pledging their support under the hashtag "how I will change." One man wrote "I will call out other men on sexism. I won't be complacent with the status quo. I won't allow another man to harass a woman."[12]

The case against Harvey Weinstein and the #MeToo campaign that followed were a watershed moment in raising to consciousness what in one sense everyone knew was going on. With women being heard rather than shamed for speaking, with women who spoke out being joined rather than abandoned by other women, and with men experiencing the consequences of actions that had long been treated as inconsequential, it is possible that collectively we are reaching the end of the tacit acceptance of this aspect of patriarchy. What from a patriarchal perspective has been a male prerogative, a spoil of war, and an accoutrement of privilege and power, when viewed through a democratic lens is a violation of human rights and an abuse of power. Put simply, the Women Wage Peace movement, the Women's March following Trump's inauguration, and the #Me Too campaign are statements on the part of a large and diverse group of women along with some men: we will no longer be complicit with patriarchy.

Why Does Patriarchy Persist?

The #MeToo campaign is not without controversy—neither is Women Wage Peace nor for that matter the unprecedented Women's March. There has been disagreement and dissent every step of the way, including about what is the best way to wage peace, who should speak under the banner of women, what constitutes harassment and abuse, and what is the appropriate response to accusations. Ironically, however, absence of conflict and disagreement is a hallmark of patriarchy, where the voice of the father is unquestioned. Totalitarian regimes brook no opposition and quickly move to silence dissent, whereas democracy thrives on open conflict and disagreement because, as Tessie knows at age eleven, airing conflict is what makes relationships go on, and it is by listening that you learn "how the person feels," and so how "not to hurt their feelings."

Where Then Do We Stand?

Carol and Naomi: We live in polarized times—in the US, we have elected the first black president, seen the first woman nominated for the presidency by a major political party, and legalized gay marriage; and yet within the same short span of years we have also heard our political leaders, including the president, endorse racism, sexism, religious intolerance, and violence, and advocate the use of force as the way to deal with conflict. We have seen powerful men stripped of their power as a consequence of having sexually abused or harassed others (mostly women), and yet the most powerful man of all—the US president—has, at the time of writing, faced no consequences for the same behavior. Patriarchy is at once under siege and in power. Given all this, where do we stand with respect to our question?

Clearly patriarchy persists, but we have a better understanding of why. The political battle between democracy and patriarchy is joined with a psychological struggle. Patriarchy's persistence is tied not only to a struggle for power and a contest between different frameworks for living or systems of belief, but also to the tension between our desire for love and our desire to avoid the pain of loss. With its gender binary and hierarchy creating impediments to relational presence and integrity, patriarchy becomes a bastion against the pain of loss. The catch is: it requires a sacrifice of love.

Two words came up repeatedly: "something"—a force felt but not named, at once massive and intangible, or in Tolstoy's description, crude, mysterious, and powerful—and "ghost": a presence from the past, dead yet hovering in our midst. We feel something acting on us, often outside our awareness or without our really noticing it, or being enacted by us without a conscious thought; we feel a ghost-like presence. Like Hamlet's father, a voice speaks to us out of the fog, telling us what we should do.

Gender is at the heart of the story because it is the foundation of patriarchy: the gender binary and hierarchy structure the order of living whereby a man, in order to be a man, must not be a woman or like a woman, and vice versa, and where some men, the patriarchs, rise to the top because, or so the story goes, they are superior to other men, and also to women. But gender—the man/woman binary and the hierarchy that elevates the masculine over the feminine—is also at the heart of the matter because it is gender that holds patriarchy in place. More precisely, it is the patriarchal construction of what it takes to be an honorable man or a good woman, because morality, or a form of morality invested in masculine honor and feminine goodness, is key to establishing and maintaining a patriarchal order. It is in the name of manhood or womanhood and for the sake of honor or goodness that the move to repair relationship is shamed and the path from protest to detachment is set.

But love—that force of nature—sneaks under the walls.

It's no secret that patriarchy depends on women's complicity. The persistence of patriarchy is premised in part on women's silence and women's compliance, including women's willingness to continue sacrificing children to whatever higher purpose or cause. It also hinges—and as the psychiatrists James Gilligan and Jonathan Shay remind us, we've known this since Homer—on men's susceptibility to a dynamic of shame and violence that can lead them, in Shay's words, to betray what's right.[1] In the Women's March following Trump's inauguration, in Women Wage Peace's 2017 journey to reconciliation, in the #MeToo movement and the silence-breaking women singled out by *Time* magazine for their 2017 person of the year cover,[2] we see women leaving patriarchy, and also men who, by the very act of joining a women's movement, have released their manhood from the vise of the gender binary and hierarchy. We see men and women joining across sharp

lines of division (Israeli/Palestinian, black/white, rich/
poor, gay/straight) to protest losses—the losses of war,
the losses associated with Trump's election, the losses
sustained over decades of abuse and racism, inequality
and sexism. We see movements fueled by the anger
of hope: the hope that things will in fact change,
that the ruptures in democracy can be repaired, that
relationship—however tenuous its hold, however beset
by appeals to masculine honor and feminine goodness—
does not give way to dominance and submission,
violence and silence. These are movements inspired
by the conviction that as humans we are capable of
reconciliation, that the moral arc of the universe bends
toward justice, and that in the end the anger of hope
will win out over the anger of despair.

At this turning point then—with patriarchy both
under siege and in power—we bring our inquiry to a
close. Looking back to where we began, what can we
learn from Jackie and Adam?

In the wake of Trump's election, in the resonant
space of the resisting injustice seminar, Adam, a straight
white man headed for a career in law, and Jackie, a
biracial straight women who attended an elite college
and worked at top-tiered educational institutions before
entering graduate school, protested a loss they had
suffered. Embracing a framework of patriarchy and
manhood, Adam had broken his true bond with Ollie,
his best friend since childhood. Recognizing that in
doing so he had betrayed not only Ollie but also himself
in his willingness to sacrifice love for a patriarchal
definition of manhood, he saw it as "possibly the single
greatest regret in my life thus far."

Jackie had silenced her honest voice. By not speaking her truth, she had abandoned herself and also absented herself from her relationships. In her final paper for the resisting injustice seminar, she describes her silence following her rape as "a betrayal of everything I had ever believed in":

> For me, the hardest thing about my rape was the silence that came after. It felt like a betrayal of everything I had ever believed in. A year before my own assault, I had learned that my friend was raped by a (former) mutual friend. I confronted the rapist, I stood by my friend's side, I connected her with resources and accompanied her to a trusted professor. At first, I could not do any of those things when it came to my own experience. I felt like I was drowning, the feeling of helplessness and the lack of ability to speak my truth.

Loss of voice is a legacy of trauma because trauma renders voice ineffective. Protest is overridden or ignored, leading to despair and detachment, including the experience of leaving one's body that is common among rape survivors. But as Jackie came to see, her silence was not only a legacy of her rape, it also served to hold patriarchy in place.

> If women remain silent then we can't build off our shared cultural experience of being lesser than. We also don't grow and learn from one another, we can't explore how the intersection of other identities affects the issues we all face. Our combined silence becomes complicit in allowing patriarchy to remain the status quo.

Perhaps the deepest lesson we learn from Adam and Jackie is that the act of resistance is at once an act of protest and a move to repair. Resisting injustice means protesting patriarchy, which is antithetical to democratic institutions and values (equal voice, human rights) but it also means repairing the ruptures in human connection, it means replacing "relationships" with relationship.

By opening ourselves (again) to what, barring extreme conditions, we knew from the beginning, at least to some extent—namely, the pleasures of engaging responsively with others—we open ourselves once again to hope for relationship and to despair should that hope be dashed. This can set in motion a defensive psychology that leads back to despair and detachment, but it also can take us on a path leading out of patriarchy. It can take us on the equivalent of the march through the desert.

As part of his end-of-term project, Adam wrote and sang a song to Ollie. He had turned to music—another love he had abandoned—to repair the rupture: "For this project I wanted to use music as a means to repair the moral injury that I suffered in 'developing' from a boy into a man." His hope in doing so was "to reconnect, at least to some small degree, my mind and my emotions," and to repair his relationship with Ollie by creating and singing "an original song confessing my lack of empathy and morality toward my best friend growing up, and my fear of public opinion for being too closely associated with a gay boy." Through reconnecting with his love for music and for Ollie, Adam took a stand against patriarchy that went beyond what

139

we usually think of as political action by engaging the psychological forces that are implicated in patriarchy's perpetuation. His song to Ollie was his repudiation of a manhood founded on a betrayal of love.

In her paper Jackie describes her decision to write her rapist a letter. In it she articulates her anger at him and maps out "the ways that I had ultimately protected him at the expense of myself." Jackie's rapist replied, admitting what he had done and how badly he felt. "My rage only grew." Jackie explains:

> A part of me before the letter had wanted to believe that he didn't fully understand what he had done to me, but his response made clear to me that this was not the case. [He knew he had raped her.] After his email, I couldn't stop thinking—if he truly felt the way he said he did in the letter, then why hadn't he apologized sooner? Why didn't he go get help? Why was I still hearing about his mistreatment of women? My silence was broken.

By protesting the injustice of her rape and also the betrayals that followed, Jackie had broken her silence. She had found a way to move back into relationship with herself and other women. With her letter, she had reached out to her rapist, who prior to raping her had been a friend. On the face of it, her response to his email may seem puzzling. He had apologized to her for the rape and said he felt guilty for what he had done. What more did she want?, one might ask.

Yet closely listened to, Jackie is asking a different question: if in fact he did "fully understand what he had done to me," then the question becomes not simply will he apologize or does he feel guilty but how could he have done it? How could he have raped her? If he was in fact not a monster but capable of human feelings, if he was in fact able to understand her feelings, then what had happened to him? What had enabled him to override his humanity including his understanding of other people's feelings? How could he have been capable not only of raping her (for which he had apologized and felt guilty) but also of continuing his mistreatment of women, as she had learned from other women? Jackie's silence was broken in part we suspect because she had come to a more systemic understanding of what had happened to her: it was not simply that Tom was a monster; Tom had done something monstrous because "something"—again that word—had separated him from his humanity.

Through their stories, told in the context of a seminar on resisting injustice, Adam and Jackie remind us to pay attention to the way things are framed. Viewed through a patriarchal lens, Tom's apology should have assuaged Jackie's rage, rather than fueling it. Seen through a feminist lens, Jackie's rage grew from her realization that in fact Tom had done nothing to confront himself or change his behavior toward women; his apology in this sense was hollow. Had she simply accepted his apology she would have entered into what within herself she knew to be a false relationship with him. But in part, and here is the deeper insight, she did not accept his apology because she realized that he was in a false relationship with himself. And this in turn was Adam's realization: his remorse was not only for having betrayed his friendship with Ollie; it was also in the realization that in betraying that true bond, that brotherly love he had felt, he had also betrayed himself. In composing and singing a song to Ollie, Adam had reclaimed his love of music and singing and of Ollie, and by doing so, come back into a truer relationship with himself.

The move from detachment to protest, from a pathological resistance to knowing to a healthy resistance to false relationship, brought Jackie into political resistance. She had come up against the "social expectation for me to grit my teeth and bear it." In taking on the forces that had silenced her, Jackie became curious about the systems that allow rape to continue, in part by their implication in women's silence. How do university administrators live with themselves, she wondered, when—according to available statistics on the continuing high rates of sexual assault on college campuses—the policies they are implementing have had little or no effect? From her own experience as well as the experiences of other women, she knew that the responses of the university administrators to whom they reported their rapes had only compounded the trauma by contributing to their self-silencing. Yet having been a university administrator herself in the time between college and graduate school, she also knew that administrators are not monsters, cold-hearted bureaucrats devoid of human feelings. How do they understand what they are doing, their role in implementing Title IX policies, their responses to students who come to them with complaints? How do they live with themselves? For her dissertation research, she will pursue these questions by interviewing university administrators responsible for reducing the incidence of sexual assault on campus.

"The rape did what nothing had before—it silenced me," Jackie had written in her final paper for the resisting injustice seminar. Her paper began, "For my sisters ... ." She was writing for her younger sisters growing up in a world where "sexual violence was something that happened and that we would have to live with," and also for the larger sisterhood of women, because she had "vowed in that detective's office [with its files of unprosecuted rapes] to never be silent again ... [about] situations of gender inequality and violence."

We began with a question: why does patriarchy persist? It led us to a set of discoveries connecting the persistence of patriarchy to the psychology of loss. The persistence of patriarchy is contingent on the move from protest to despair and detachment. Otherwise we would all be up in arms.

We end with a realization. Within the very psychology that sustains patriarchy are the seeds for resistance and transformation. Because we live in what is in many ways a dark time, the anger of hope becomes a beacon, showing us a way out of despair.

Naomi: For me the key insight was that loss, which separates us, also connects us. With this realization I began to see how, despite the forces operating against it, repair is always possible, loss is never irrevocable.

Carol: For me, it was the realization of how precise the mechanism is that holds patriarchy in place. Like clockwork, patriarchy strikes shame at the moves to repair the ruptures that stand in the way of democracy and love. Patriarchy strikes at the heart of what makes repair possible: our sensitivity to the pain of losing connection and our ability to give voice to what we are experiencing.

We kept circling back to the baby in the YouTube video to remind ourselves that these are human capacities, present from the very outset of life.

Carol and Naomi: We come then to the recognition that political change depends on psychological transformation and vice versa. Leaving the psychology of patriarchy intact, we are unlikely to get rid of its politics. Leaving its politics in place, its psychology is easily mistaken for nature. Men appear emotionally clueless, incapable of registering their own hurt or that of others; women are deemed preternaturally selfless, angels, or if not angels, then sluts.

In the process of writing together, we noticed that we had become sounding boards for one another, picking up what was often just a faint resonance and discovering that by giving voice to our doubts or questions, to our curiosity or understanding, we could call forth in the other something that had felt unsayable. We marveled at how little it could take to shift the resonance and, by doing so, free a voice that had been tied up in confusion or held in silence. Upon reflection this experience brings home to us the forces marshaled against this happening within the wider human community. Because if, as our work suggests, there is a fundamental tension between the human response to loss and the structures that depend on loss becoming irreparable, this is where the battle will be engaged.

Where Then Do We Stand?

Put simply, patriarchy is contingent on subverting the human capacity to repair relationship: its hierarchy is premised on a loss of relationship and thereby on a sacrifice of love. Conversely, democracy, like love, is contingent on relationship: on everyone having a voice that is grounded in their experience. In this sense, everyone's voice is recognized as essential to the realization of democratic processes and values and therefore both called forth and welcomed, heard and responded to—not necessarily with agreement, but with respect. Equal voice is the condition that makes it possible to work through conflicts in relationship without the use of force or by other means of domination. The relational capacities that constitute our humanity stand at the crossroads of where we have come to collectively, at this volatile intersection of democracy and patriarchy. And the question that confronts us, that confounds us perhaps more urgently now than ever before, is: which way will we go?

Notes

Introduction

1 A. Roy, *The God of Small Things*, New Delhi: India Ink, 2001/1997, p. 33.
2 L. Tolstoy, *Anna Karenina*, trans. R. Pevear and L. Volokhonsky, New York: Penguin, 2001/1878, p. 418.
3 Ibid., p. 419.
4 Ibid., p. 425.
5 T. Sidesinger, "The Nasty Woman: Destruction and the Path to Mutual Recognition," conference paper, "Psychology & the Other," Boston, October 13–15, 2017.
6 See e.g., F. De Waal, *The Age of Empathy*, New York: Harmony, 2009; M. D. Lieberman, *Social: Why Our Brains are Wired to Connect*, New York: Random House, 2013; S. Hrdy, *Mothers and Others*, Cambridge, MA: Belknap Press of Harvard University Press, 2011; N. Way, A. Ali., C. Gilligan, and P. Noguera, eds, *Crisis of Connection:*

Its Roots, Consequences, and Solutions, New York: NYU Press, 2018.

7 Hrdy, *Mothers and Others*, p. 287.

8 D. Ackerman, *The Zookeeper's Wife*, New York: W. W. Norton & Co., 2007. A. Lori, "Code Name: Fox," *Haaretz*, February 21, 2008, https://www.haaretz.com/1.4994531 (accessed May 2, 2018). See also P. Hallie, *Lest Innocent Blood be Shed: The Story of the Village of Le Chambon and How Goodness Happened There*, New York: Harper and Row, 1979; B. Lidegaard, *Countrymen: The Untold Story of How Denmark's Jews Escaped the Nazis, of the Courage of Their Fellow Danes and of the Extraordinary Role of the SS*, New York: Alfred A. Knopf, 2013.

9 Available at https://www.youtube.com/watch?v=apzXGEbZht0 (accessed January 11, 2018).

10 S. Freud, "The Question of Lay Analysis," in *The Standard Edition of the Complete Psychological Works of Sigmund Freud*, Vol. 20, ed. and trans. J. Strachey, London: Hogarth Press, 1959/26, pp. 222–3.

The Puzzle

1 C. Gilligan, *The Birth of Pleasure*, New York: Alfred A. Knopf, 2002.

2 Ibid., p. 10.

3 See C. Gilligan, "The Centrality of Relationship in Human Development: A Puzzle, Some Evidence, and a Theory," in K. Fisher and G. Noam, eds, *Development and Vulnerability in Close*

Relationships, New Jersey: Lawrence Erlbaum Associates, 1996; S. Nolen-Hoeksema, J. S. Girgus, and M. E. Seligman, "Sex Differences in Depression and Explanatory Style in Children," *Journal of Youth and Adolescence*, 20(2), 1991, pp. 233–45.

4　J. Y. Chu, *When Boys Become Boys: Development, Relationships, and Masculinity*, New York: New York University Press, 2014.

5　Ibid., pp. 26–7.

6　Ibid., p. 206.

7　Ibid., pp. 203–7.

8　N. Way, *Deep Secrets: Boys' Friendships and the Crisis of Connection*, Cambridge, MA: Harvard University Press, 2011.

9　Ibid., p. 1.

10　Ibid., p. 242.

11　Apuleius, *Metamorphoses* (second century CE), trans. J. A. Hanson, Cambridge, MA: Harvard University Press, 1989.

12　Sophocles, *The Oedipus Cycle* (429 BCE), trans. D. Fitts and D. R. Fitzgerald, New York: Harcourt, Brace & World, 1949.

13　Ibid., pp. 66, 56.

The First Clue: An Association to Loss

1　Gilligan, *The Birth of Pleasure*, p. 65.

Resistance

1 C. Gilligan, *Joining the Resistance*, Cambridge: Polity Press, 2011, p. 63.
2 A. Phillips, "Judas' Gift," *London Review of Books*, January 5, 2012, p. 14.
3 Shakespeare, *The Tempest*, ed. R. Langbaum, New York: Penguin, 1998, 4.1:106.
4 Gilligan, *Joining the Resistance*, p. 66.
5 L. M. Brown and C. Gilligan, *Meeting at the Crossroads: Women's Psychology and Girls' Development*, Cambridge, MA: Harvard University Press, 1992, p. 137.
6 A. R. Damasio, *Descartes' Error: Emotion, Reason and the Human Brain*, New York: Putnam Publishing Group, 1994; A. R. Damasio, *The Feeling of What Happens: Body and Emotion in the Making of Consciousness*, San Diego: Harcourt, 1999.
7 Brown and Gilligan, *Meeting at the Crossroads*, p. 138.
8 Way, *Deep Secrets*, p. 2.
9 Brown and Gilligan, *Meeting at the Crossroads*, p. 40.
10 L. Machoian, *The Disappearing Girl: Learning the Language of Teenage Depression*, New York: Penguin, 2006, pp. 40–1.
11 Gilligan, *Joining the Resistance*, pp. 134–5.

Loss

1 S. Freud, "Mourning and Melancholia," in *The Standard Edition of the Complete Psychological*

Works of Sigmund Freud, Vol. 14, ed. and trans. J. Strachey, London: Hogarth Press, 1957/17, pp. 237–58.

2 Ibid., p. 249.

3 M. Klein, "A Contribution to the Psychogenesis of Manic-Depressive States," *International Journal of Psycho-Analysis*, 16, 1935, pp. 145–74.

4 J. Bowlby, *Attachment and Loss*, 3 vols, New York: Basic Books, 1969, 1973, 1980.

5 Bowlby, *Attachment and Loss, Vol. 1*, pp. 27–8.

6 Ibid., p. 27.

7 Bowlby, *Attachment and Loss, Vol. 2*, p. 246.

8 Ibid., pp. 201–2. "Only when an attachment figure is both accessible and potentially responsive can he, or she, be said to be truly available. In what follows, therefore, the word 'available' is to be understood as implying that an attachment figure is both accessible and responsive."

9 For discussion of the distinctions between democracy and authoritarianism see Gilligan, *Joining the Resistance*; C. Gilligan and D. A. J. Richards, *The Deepening Darkness: Patriarchy, Resistance, and Democracy's Future*, Cambridge: Cambridge University Press, 2008; C. Gilligan and D. A. J. Richards, *Darkness Now Visible: Patriarchy's Resurgence and Feminist Resistance*, Cambridge: Cambridge University Press, forthcoming.

10 Bowlby's discoveries initiated a wave of reform of hospitalization practices in pediatric wards, including extended visiting hours and the inclusion of beds for parents. For an overview of this impact see R. Kozlovsky, *The Architects of Childhood: Childhood, Modern Architecture,*

and Reconstruction in Postwar England, New York: Routledge, 2016, pp. 141–72; H. Hendrick, "Children's Emotional Well-being and Mental Health in Early Post-Second World War Britain: The Case of Unrestricted Hospital Visiting," *Cultures of Child Health in Britain and the Netherlands in the Twentieth Century*, 17, 2003.

11 Bowlby, *Attachment and Loss, Vol. 1*, pp. 27–8.

12 Bowlby, *Attachment and Loss, Vol. 2*, pp. 246–57.

13 Ibid., p. 248.

14 Ibid., p. 249.

15 Ibid., p. 250.

16 S. H. Sands, "What is Dissociated?," *Dissociation: Progress in the Dissociative Disorders*, 7, 1994, pp. 145–52, p. 149.

17 Bowlby, *Attachment and Loss, Vol. 1*, p. 28.

18 Ibid., emphasis added.

19 Bowlby, *Attachment and Loss, Vol. 3*, pp. 369–70.

20 Bowlby, *Attachment and Loss, Vol. 2*, p. 19.

21 Bowlby, *Attachment and Loss, Vol. 3*, p. 70. "The deactivation of systems mediating attachment behaviour, thought and feeling, appears to be achieved by the defensive exclusion, more or less complete, of sensory inflow of any and every kind that might activate attachment behaviour and feeling. The resulting state is one of emotional detachment which can be either partial or complete."

22 A. D. Smith, *Notes From the Field*, directed by L. Foglia, Second Stage Theatre, New York, November 2, 2016.

23 J. Bowlby, "On Knowing What You Are Not Supposed to Know and Feeling What You Are Not

Supposed to Feel," *Can. J. Psychiatry*, 24(5), 1979, pp. 403–8.

24 Ibid., p. 406.

25 Way, *Deep Secrets*, p. 231.

26 Ibid., p. 233.

27 Ibid.

28 Ibid., p. 232.

29 Ibid., p. 241.

30 Ibid., p. 242.

31 Ibid., p. 241.

32 P. M. Bromberg makes this point with respect to the replacement of relationships with food in the case of eating disordered patients. See P. M. Bromberg, "Treating Patients with Symptoms—and Symptoms with Patience," *Psychoanalytic Dialogues*, 11(6), 2001, pp. 891–912.

33 Way, *Deep Secrets*, p. 189.

34 Ibid., p. 193.

35 J. Gilligan, *Violence: Reflections on a National Epidemic*, New York: Vintage Books, 1996.

36 Bowlby, *Attachment and Loss, Vol. 2*, pp. 211–15.

37 For overview of compulsive caregiving see Bowlby, *Attachment and Loss, Vol. 3*, pp. 156–7, 206–11, 222–4, and for further discussion of anxious attachment, pp. 203–6, 218–22.

38 D. C. Jack, *Silencing the Self: Women and Depression*, Cambridge MA: Harvard University Press, 1991, p. 40. *Silencing the Self* provides an understanding of depression in women, which ties the higher rates of depression in women to social factors attached to women's social inequality. For an international examination of this theory of depression and a cross-cultural understanding of

how internalized cultural expectations of feminine goodness affect women's behavior and their experience of depression see D. C. Jack and A. Ali, eds, *Silencing the Self Across Cultures: Depression and Gender in the Social World*, Oxford: Oxford University Press, 2010.

39 Bowlby, *Attachment and Loss, Vol. 3*, p. 157.
40 Ibid., pp. 67–8.
41 Jack, *Silencing the Self*, p. 40.
42 Bowlby, *Attachment and Loss, Vol. 3*, pp. 69–70.
43 W. R. D. Fairbairn, *Psychoanalytic Studies of the Personality*, London: Tavistock, 1952, p. 66.
44 Bowlby, *Attachment and Loss, Vol. 3*, p. 71; see also Bowlby, "On Knowing."
45 V. Woolf, "Professions for Women," in *The Death of the Moth and Other Essays*, New York: Harcourt, Brace and Company, 1942/31, pp. 149–54.
46 Ibid.
47 Bowlby, *Attachment and Loss, Vol. 3*, p. 411. "In terms of the theory advanced here the behaviour in question is to be regarded as an alternative to seeking care. Because, moreover, it is a form of behaviour that is incompatible with seeking care and also because of the very fact that it does bring some measure of comfort, and is often highly approved by grownups, there is always risk that caregiving of others will be resorted to routinely whenever seeking care for the self would be the appropriate response."
48 J. Holmes, *Attachment, Intimacy, Autonomy: Using Attachment Theory in Adult Psychotherapy*, New Jersey: Rowman & Littlefield, 1996, p. 100.

The Three Discoveries

1 Damasio, *Descartes' Error*; Damasio, *The Feeling of What Happens*; J. E. LeDoux, *The Emotional Brain*, New York: Simon & Schuster, 1996.

2 Brown and Gilligan, *Meeting at the Crossroads*, p. 119.

3 E. Dickinson, "Poem 670" (1863, excerpted), in *The Complete Poems of Emily Dickinson*, ed. T. H. Johnson, Boston, MA: Little, Brown, 1960, p. 333.

4 D. Barnow, H. Paape, and G. Van Der Stroom, eds, *The Diary of Anne Frank: The Revised Critical Edition Prepared by The Netherlands Institute for War Documentation*, trans. Arnold J. Pomerans and B. M. Mooyaart, New York: Doubleday/Random House, 2003, pp. 719, 721.

5 D. Umberson and J. Karas Montez, "Social Relationships and Health: A Flashpoint for Health Policy," *Journal of Health and Social Behavior*, 51(1 supplement), 2010, pp. S54–S66; G. Bosmans and B. De Smedt, "Insecure Attachment is Associated with Math Anxiety in Middle Childhood," *Frontiers in Psychology*, 6, 2012, p. 1596.

6 b. hooks, "Understanding Patriarchy," 2013, Louisville Anarchist Federation, Louisville Lending Library, 2003.

7 Ibid., p. 2.

8 Ibid., p. 1.

9 Ibid.

10 Gilligan, *Joining the Resistance*, p. 132.

11 V. L. Brescoll and E. L. Uhlmann, "Can an Angry Woman Get Ahead? Status Conferral, Gender,

and Expression of Emotion in the Workplace," *Psychological Science*, 19(3), 2008, pp. 268–75.

12 See e.g. M. Morris, *Pushout: The Criminalization of Black Girls in Schools*, New York: The New Press, 2015; A. Ritchie and A. Y. Davis, *Invisible No More: Police Violence Against Black Women and Women of Color*, Boston: Beacon Press, 2017.

13 T. G. Okimoto and V. L. Brescoll, "The Price of Power: Power Seeking and Backlash Against Female Politicians," *Personality and Social Psychology Bulletin*, 36(7), 2010, pp. 923–36.

14 Quoted by R. Traister, "Hillary Clinton Is Furious. And Resigned. And Funny. And Worried," *New York Magazine*, May 26, 2017, http://nymag.com/daily/intelligencer/2017/05/hillary-clinton-life-after-election.html (accessed January 14, 2018).

15 When Clinton stepped down as US secretary of State in January 2013 her approval rating was 69%, rendering her the most popular politician in the country and the second most popular secretary of state since 1948. See S. Doyle, "America Loves Women Like Hillary Clinton—As Long As They're Not Asking For a Promotion," *Quartz*, February 25, 2016, https://qz.com/624346/america-loves-women-like-hillary-clinton-as-long-as-theyre-not-asking-for-a-promotion (accessed January 15, 2018).

16 M. Beard, *Women & Power: A Manifesto*, New York: W. W Norton & Company, 2017.

17 Way, *Deep Secrets*, pp. 220–1.

18 Ibid., p. 92.

19 Ibid., p. 93.

20 Ibid., p. 1.

21 Ibid., p. 209.
22 D. Jack, "The Anger of Hope and the Anger of Despair: How Anger Relates to Women's Depression," in J. M. Stoppard and L. M. McMullen, eds, *Situating Sadness: Women and Depression in Social Context*, New York: NYU Press, 2003, pp. 62–87.
23 Ibid., p. 65.
24 Ibid.
25 Way, *Deep Secrets*, pp. 185, 189.
26 Ibid., p. 222. This aggressive rage tends to be directed outward. However, in extreme situations violent rage is redirected against the self—a phenomenon reflected in the epidemic rates of male suicide.
27 Ibid., p. 113.

Knowing This, Then What?

1 C. Gilligan, "Recovering Psyche," *The Annual of Psychoanalysis, V. 32: Psychoanalysis and Women*, 32, 2013, pp. 131–48, at p. 134.
2 For a more comprehensive overview of the intersections between race and gender see P. H. Collins, *Black Feminist Thought: Knowledge, Consciousness, and the Politics of Empowerment*, New York: Routledge, 2000; P. H. Collins and S. Bilge, *Intersectionality*, Cambridge: Polity, 2016; K. Crenshaw et al., eds, *Critical Race Theory: The Key Writings That Formed the Movement*, New York: The New Press, 1996; K-Y. Taylor, *How We Get Free: Black Feminism and the Combahee River Collective*, Chicago: Haymarket Books, 2017.

3 J. Adelson and M. Doehrman, "The Psychodynamic Approach to Adolescence," in J. Adelson, ed., *Handbook of Adolescent Psychology*, New York: Wiley, 1980, p. 114.

4 Ibid.

5 Gilligan, *Birth of Pleasure*, p. 9.

6 C. H. Sommers, "The War Against Boys," *The Atlantic*, May 2000, https://www.theatlantic.com/magazine/archive/2000/05/the-war-against-boys/304659 (accessed January 14, 2018).

7 C. Gilligan, *In a Different Voice*, Cambridge, MA: Harvard University Press, 1982, p. 2.

8 Brown and Gilligan, *Meeting at the Crossroads*, p. 5.

9 P. C. Davis, *Neglected Stories*, New York: Hill and Wang, 1998.

10 D. A. J. Richards, *Women, Gays, and the Constitution: The Grounds for Feminism and Gay Rights in Culture and Law*, Chicago: University of Chicago Press, 1998.

11 For discussion of patriarchy as a threat to democracy see also Gilligan and Richards, *The Deepening Darkness*, and *Darkness Now Visible*.

12 Gilligan, *Birth of Pleasure*, p. 6.

13 Ibid., p. 53.

14 Ibid.

15 See J. A. Dorney, "Splitting the World Open: Connection and Disconnection Among Women Teaching Girls," in N. Way et al., *Crisis of Connection: Its Roots, Consequences, and Solutions*, New York: NYU Press, 2018.

Leaving Patriarchy

1 UNSC Res 1325 (October 31, 2000) UN Doc S/RES/1325.

2 D. Kirshbaum, "Why Women and Why Now?," womenwagepeace, June 2, 2017, http://womenwagepeace.org.il/en/women-now-rabbi-donna-kirshbaum-member-women-wage-peace (accessed January 15, 2018).

3 O. Lieberman, "Israeli, Palestinian Women Join Peace March Through Desert," *CNN*, October 9, 2017, http://www.cnn.com/2017/10/09/middleeast/israeli-palestinian-women-peace-march-desert/index.html (accessed January 16, 2018).

4 Ibid.

5 Kirshbaum, "Why Women and Why Now?"

6 Ibid.

7 The Radical Listening Project, NYU, https://wp.nyu.edu/radicallisteningproject.

8 J. Kantor and M. Twohey, "Harvey Weinstein Paid Off Sexual Harassment Accusers for Decades," *New York Times*, October 5, 2017, https://www.nytimes.com/2017/10/05/us/harvey-weinstein-harassment-allegations.html?_r=0 (accessed January 15, 2018).

9 Z. Hill, "A Black Woman Created the 'Me Too' Campaign Against Sexual Assault 10 Years Ago," *Ebony*, October 18, 2017, http://www.ebony.com/news-views/black-woman-me-too-movement-tarana-burke-alyssa-milano#ixzz54I5qwqoZ (accessed January 15, 2018).

10 A. Milano, "If you've been sexually harassed or assaulted write 'me too' as a reply to this

tweet," October 15, 2017, https://twitter.com/ Alyssa_Milano/status/919659438700670976?ref_ src=twsrc%5Etfw&ref_url=http%3A%2F%2 Fwww.cnn.com%2F2017%2F10%2F15% 2Fentertainment%2Fme-too-twitter-alyssa- milano%2Findex.html (accessed January 15, 2018).

11 A. Park, "#MeToo Reaches 85 Countries With 1.7M Tweets," *CBS News*, October 24, 2017, https://www. cbsnews.com/news/o-reaches-85-countries-with- 1-7-million-tweets (accessed January 15, 2018).

12 A. Vagianos, "In Response to #MeToo, Men Are Tweeting #HowIWillChange," *Huffington Post*, October 18, 2017, https://www.huffingtonpost. com/entry/in-response-to-metoo-men-are-tweeting- howiwillchange_us_59e79bd3e4b00905bdae455d (accessed January 15, 2018).

Where Then Do We Stand?

1 Gilligan, *Violence*; J. Shay, *Achilles in Vietnam: Combat Trauma and the Undoing of Character*, New York: Simon and Schuster, 1994.

2 S. Zackerek, E. Docterman, and H. S. Edwards, "The Silence Breakers," *Time*, December 18, 2017, http://time.com/time-person-of-the-year-2017- silence-breakers (accessed January 15, 2018).

INDEX

INDEX

INDEX